THE
POCKET
DOCTOR

A PASSPORT TO HEALTHY TRAVEL

3RD EDITION

Stephen Bezruchka, M.D., MPH

THE
MOUNTAINEERS

Published by
The Mountaineers
1001 SW Klickitat Way, Suite 201
Seattle, WA 98134

© 1988, 1992, 1999 by Stephen Bezruchka

First edition 1988. Second edition 1992. Third edition: first
printing 1999, revised 2000, revised 2005

Published simultaneously in Great Britain by Cordee,
3a DeMontfort Street, Leicester, England, LE1 7HD

Manufactured in Canada

Edited by Kris Fulsaas
Cover design by Kristy L. Welch
Book design and layout by Peggy Egerdahl

Library of Congress Cataloging-in-Publication Data
Bezruchka, Stephen.
   The pocket doctor : a passport to healthy travel / Stephen
Bezruchka. — 3rd ed.
       p.   cm.
   Includes bibliographical references.
   ISBN 0-89886-614-6
   1. Travel—Health aspects—Handbooks, manuals, etc. I. Title.
RA783.5.B49 1999
613.6'8—dc21   98-52801
                                                              CIP

 Printed on recycled paper

CONTENTS

PREFACE

Whether you are going on a 3-day holiday to Hawaii, a three-week tour of Europe, or a three-month trek through Inner Asia, understanding the hazards of the trip and the limits of one's body will help travelers adapt and enjoy the journey more. *The Pocket Doctor* attempts to provide you with the information to stay healthy and to deal initially with health problems. Feel free to send suggestions for improvement of this book as well as practical ideas that worked for you to the author, in care of the publisher. Endorsement of any products other than this book and others I have written is devoid of any financial interest on my part.

Acknowledgments

Thanks to Howard Backer, Peter Banys, Rachel Bishop, Elaine Jong, Jay Keystone, Alfred Lewy, Mary Anne Mercer, Karl Neumann, Geoff Newman-Martin, John Sinsky, and Zu Horowitz Smith for your comments and suggestions for improvement. Kris Fulsaas has helped improve this edition with her fine editing. I continue to learn much from users of this book.

INTRODUCTION

This book attempts to provide the traveler with the essential information to prepare for a trip, to stay healthy along the journey, and to initiate care of health problems that might arise en route. Other books deal with this subject, but they are all large volumes whose size makes it less likely that they will be taken along to refresh one's memory when needed. Many volumes have well-meaning advice applicable to a clinical setting or a modern hotel, but of little use in, say, Humla, Nepal, or Iquitos, Peru. I have tried to deal with most settings. I don't always tell you why to do things, just what to do. Prevention is emphasized where specific practical suggestions can be given. The suggestions in this book are directed toward common problems encountered by travelers, and so warrant serious consideration. If the problem you have is not reviewed in this book, it is because either I can give no practical recommendation or it is rare in travelers. For more information, consult the works listed in Recommended Reading at the back of this book.

Material dealing with strictly classical survival topics such as being adrift on the ocean, lost in the desert, or the lone survivor of a mountaineering accident is not covered. The interested reader should consult specialized works on the subjects, especially if planning to be involved in such activities.

Compliance with suggested regimens to prevent and treat travel-related disorders is quite poor among the following groups: the young, those on long trips, experienced travelers, individual travelers, and especially those visiting friends and relatives. Increased vigilance is appropriate if you fall in one of those categories.

A CAUTION

This book is not a substitute for expert advice obtained from your own doctor or someone versed in the new specialty of travel medicine. I use the term "doctor" in a generic sense. In the United States, this could be a physician, nurse practitioner, physician's assistant, or some other practitioner of the healing arts. Overseas, besides the familiar doctor, you may encounter yet other types of health-care practitioners. (The equivalent of the Chinese barefoot doctor exists in many other places.) They can provide appropriate care and refer you if need be. See chapter 2, Finding Medical Help Abroad.

Don't treat yourself or others unless there is no alternative or the problem is simple. Family members are the least qualified to treat one another. Emotions frequently confuse the issues and mistakes are more common. The same goes for health-care workers: The doctor who treats him- or herself has a fool for a patient. So seek out appropriate advice, treatment, and care using the guidelines given here. If your travels regularly take you to places where health facilities are nonexistent or hard to reach, then you should consult the more detailed sources in Recommended Reading at the back of this book, and carry the more complete medical kits mentioned in those books.

One question asked by potential travelers abroad, especially those with chronic illnesses and disabilities, is whether it is appropriate for them to journey to the particular region they have in mind. This is a complex consideration. Factors in the decision should include the person's willingness to assume risks, the type of travel, the availability of medical resources at the destination, and, perhaps most important, the determination of the traveler. The psychological benefits of pursuing your dream of a lifetime may far outweigh the risk of having a health problem en route or upon arrival that you can't deal with by dialing 911. Seek counsel from your doctor, from other experts, who more often than not may advise against it, and especially from others with your problem who have traveled to the area you wish to go to and have undertaken similar activities.

HOW TO USE THIS BOOK

Before you begin your trip, study the organization of this book so that when you need information you can find it quickly. The first three chapters focus on preparation, finding assistance, and prevention. Be sure to read these before your trip begins. The next three chapters cover specific health problems—common, less common, and life-threatening—that travelers may have to confront. Common and less common problems are both discussed in alphabetical order for quick reference. The final chapter offers health tips for the returning traveler.

INTERNET INFORMATION

I ponder the role of books as a source of helpful advice in the new information age. The Internet provides the universe's biggest haystack wherein you may find hundreds of thousands of needles, a few of which will sew for you and many others may stab or prick you. For the near future, Wi-Fi access may not be possible on many travels, and I expect continued need for small volumes such as this, where most everything you need to know is compactly presented. Some helpful sites are listed in the text and I hope they don't change soon. Common sense should always prevail. I am reminded of a colleague who perused the web looking for advice for the chest pain symptoms his wife began having. His spouse died while he was surfing.

1

BEFORE YOU GO

Think about your health when you first make plans to travel. Visit your doctor and discuss the topics covered in this chapter. If you do not have a family doctor, choose one before leaving on a trip. Obtain information, immunizations, and advice from your doctor.

The advisable immunizations usually take four to eight weeks to administer humanely. If you must leave on short notice, an abbreviated course of vaccinations can be given, provided that you can tolerate the discomfort from multiple hits to the immune system, including temporary malaise, fevers, and injection-site soreness.

In addition to your family doctor, the following resources are available for these services:

> **County Public Health Department**
> **State Public Health Department**
> **Travel clinics,** *often associated with university medical centers or public health departments, but now there are many good ones without such affiliation; you can find them in the yellow pages or by browsing in the Web resources listed below.*

Certification in travel medicine is being newly offered through the American Society of Tropical Medicine and Hygiene (ASTMH), so doctors with this credential have passed a test on their knowledge of basic information on this subject. A list of travel medicine clinics and doctors is available from ASTMH at 60 Revere Drive, Suite 500, Northbrook, IL 60062, (847) 480-9592, fax (847)480-9282, astmh@astmh.org. Its Website URL for this service is http://www.astmh.org/scripts/clinindex.asp.

The key reason for seeking out a knowledgeable practitioner of travel medicine is to get destination-specific and activity-appropriate advice for your travels. Many people needlessly take anti-malarials when their itinerary does not subject them to any risk of contracting malaria, while others are not counseled regarding specific hazards relating to the exploits they plan to undertake. Appropriate advice for the individual or group on their journey requires an amalgam of science, experience, and care.

Some European countries have instituted requirements that travel agents provide their clients with "health measures necessary for incident-free travel and stay, and information about areas with a risk for malaria." We can expect liability issues in the United States to result in travel agents and tour operators providing such information in the future.

Other preparations are not so discomforting, but every bit as essential. If you have not done so recently, take a first-aid course before you leave. Courses oriented toward mountaineering and other risky activities where help is not a phone call away teach more skills of self-reliance and are preferable.

If you plan to spend a month or more in a poor, third-world environment among the local people, have a tuberculin skin test done before you leave. This is good advice for anyone these days, when TB is re-emerging in many countries, including the United States.

Before you depart, leave a copy of your itinerary with a responsible individual. Your itinerary should include dates of departure and arrival at each destination, flight information, addresses where you will be staying, phone numbers where you can be reached, as well as a copy of your health history (described below), together with the name, address, and phone number of your local doctor. Ask your reliable contact person to accept an international collect call from you in case of an emergency. You should also leave him or her with the U.S. State Department phone numbers to contact for assistance. It might be a good idea to leave all this in duplicate with a family member and also a friend. Be sure to bring their phone numbers and addresses with you!

SOURCES OF INFORMATION ON CARE ABROAD AND ARRANGING EVACUATIONS

See chapter 2, Finding Medical Help Abroad, for information on locating medical services after arriving in a foreign country. The following organizations can provide specific information on finding emergency medical care, and English-speaking doctors, abroad:

International Association for Medical Assistance to Travelers (IAMAT), 1623 Military Road, #279, Niagara Falls, NY 14304-1745, (716) 754-4883, or 40 Regal Road, Guelph, ON, Canada N1K 1B5, (519) 836-0102, fax (519) 836-3412, E-mail info@iamat.org, Web site http://www.iamat.org/. IAMAT is a nonprofit foundation that provides lists of English-speaking doctors abroad as well as invaluable health information. Its doctors charge a fixed fee for services to members. Membership is free, though a donation is requested and I strongly advise you to support this valuable service.

International SOS Assistance, 3600 Horizon Boulevard, Suite 300, Trevose, PA 19053, (215) 942-8000 or (800) 523-8930, fax (215) 942-8299, E-mail sosphl@intsos.com, Web site http://www.intsos.com/. This organization contracts to provide medical assistance abroad.

International Society of Travel Medicine, Box 871089, Stone Mountain, GA 30087-0028, E-mail istm@istm.org, Web site http://www.istm.org. This organization publishes a clinic directory available on its web site, where there are other useful links.

The State Department's Citizens Emergency Center, (202) 647-5225, afterhours (202) 647-4000, Web site http://travel.state.gov/travel/warnings.html. The State Department may attempt to provide assistance for a U.S. citizen if a death or an arrest has occurred, emergency funds are necessary, medical help or evacuation is needed, or an individual is missing. Postings on its Web site are kept up to date on particular hazards of travel to specific countries.

Most of the traveler's insurance companies (see below) also provide assistance with finding medical assistance abroad. Be sure to understand the specifics and limitations of any service you sign on with.

Before going abroad, verify the addresses and phone numbers of any facilities listed in this book on which you might later rely.

Consul and Embassy Addresses. Obtain the addresses, phone numbers, E-mail addresses, and telex numbers of embassies and consular offices, for both your country of residence and for passport-issuing countries you will visit, before you leave home. Libraries can help you find this information and guide you to Web-based resources. These offices can be helpful if you should need medical attention abroad. Knowing where the facility is located before you arrive in a strange place can save time and limit frustration, especially if you need help in a hurry. Once you arrive in the country, check in there, register, and obtain any up-to-date health information. Take the time to meet with a consular official if your travels will take you far from the usual tourist path. He or she may have valuable advice. Most state departments encourage their citizens to check in while traveling.

Traveler's Medical Insurance. Besides the difficulties inherent in finding the right medical care during your travels, it must be paid for. Luckily, the cost of care outside the United States is usually considerably less than in this country. Evacuation costs can be enormous, however. If you have medical insurance, first determine if it will pay for care outside the United States. Even if it will, there are usually restrictions that determine if supplemental insurance is needed. Medicare usually will not cover care outside the United States. Some of the supplemental policies may. Other private companies provide health insurance specifically designed for travelers. They may help find sources of care for you, arrange evacuations, and provide immediate payment. Such a policy is recommended for older travelers.

But before you sign on, read the fine print to determine what services you are buying. Most providers overseas will not bill your insurance company; you will have to pay at the time the service is given and get reimbursed later. Some providers exclude travel to certain countries. Others will only pay for evacuation that is preauthorized by some agency. Travel agents and insurance brokers are a good source for learning about the specialized insurance companies. Most of the major credit card companies also provide travel insurance.

IMMUNIZATIONS

Most travelers to Europe, Japan, Australia, and other developed countries won't need special immunizations. However, a major preventive step for travelers to the third world is immunization.

Current information on immunization requirements and disease prevalences for specific countries is maintained in the annual publication *Health Information for International Travel (HIFIT)*. Travelers are urged to consult this booklet to learn of the potential disease hazards facing them when they travel to a specific locale. This information is not included in this book because areas of chloroquine-resistant malaria and disease prevalence change periodically. Even more current information on epidemics and health conditions is provided by county and state public health departments that subscribe to the biweekly *Summary of Health Information for International Travel*. This supplement is issued by the Center for Disease Control and Prevention to provide updated yellow fever vaccination requirements.

The CDC also offers an up-to-date voice information system hotline for both physicians and travelers, and can fax the material to you immediately. Call (877) 395-8747 for international travel information. Updated country information on malaria, yellow fever, Japanese encephalitis, and plague is available. Online information is available at http://www.cdc.gov/travel/. This includes the entire *HIFIT*, which may be downloaded in a pdf or hypertext file.

There is a corresponding publication, *International Travel and Health* by the World Health Organization (WHO), which offers similar advice. It is available on the Internet at http://www.who.int/ith/.

Keep track of your immunizations by recording them on a yellow *International Certificate of Vaccination* when they are administered. This WHO-approved form is issued by state and local health departments, and by travel clinics. Yellow fever vaccinations must be officially recorded and stamped. These may be necessary to enter certain countries. Immigrations officials may ask for proof and can prevent your entry there if your certificate is not produced and properly completed. Countries in Africa and Asia can sometimes institute cholera vaccination requirements for entry at a moment's notice, thus limiting your mobility if you do not have this immunization. You might wish to consider this vaccine for that reason. A single dose is sufficient to satisfy this regulation.

Pre-exposure rabies vaccination is available via several products used in different dosages over a month. The new tissue culture vaccines produce far fewer reactions than older preparations that may still be available in many countries. If you're later bitten by a potentially rabid animal, you still need two further doses of vaccine, although there may be an additional safety factor in extending the deadline for these. If not vaccinated, you need five doses of vaccine over a month, plus Rabies Immune Globulin (RIG), costing perhaps $3,000. RIG is not available in many countries so being bitten usually necessitates expensive travel to a site where it can be administered. Adventure travelers to rural, remote areas should get this costly prevention. Once immunized you may not need booster doses.

Other diseases that are very rare among travelers, for which there are vaccines available, include Japanese encephalitis. Few cases have been reported in Americans and the risk of acquiring this potentially devastating disease is very low, except for travelers in some rural areas at times of high risk. The vaccine has serious potential side effects but may be appropriate for certain travelers.

For pregnant women, infants, and children under two years of age, refer to *Health Information for International Travel* regarding immunization procedures; it is also an excellent source of up-to-date information on vaccines.

Hepatitis A is the most important vaccine that is neglected by travelers.

Individuals with an altered immune response should not receive live vaccines. People with AIDS and certain cancers fall in this category. In Table 2, Immunizations, indications are given as to which vaccines use live viruses. Consult with your doctor. A mild illness, breast feeding, someone pregnant in the household, or taking an antibiotic are not contraindications to getting most vaccines.

All immunizations cause some discomfort; rarely, some people are allergic to them. Table 2, Immunizations, is detailed to help you ensure adequate protection. Travelers whose schedule prevents them from completing the immunization series in time may elect to have an abbreviated schedule. Consult with your doctor.

DENTAL CARE

If your travels will take you to remote places for an extended period of time, visit your dentist well before departure if you anticipate problems, and shortly beforehand if your dental hygiene is fine. Recent (within 24 hours) dental work, dental caries, and loose fillings can cause pain for a traveler in an unpressurized aircraft or when scuba diving.

DRUGS

"Drugs are for research and for sale, not for taking."
—*my pharmacology professor*

Remember that drugs, though valuable, are not the cure-all.

The drugs you might carry on your journey depend on your state of health, your anxiety level, the region you will be traveling to, and the activities you plan to undertake there. If medical care is easily available, then it is prudent to limit your selection. However, an extended choice is offered in Table 3, Drug Doses and Information. The list given is not exhaustive by any means. There are many other items one could include. Select what might be appropriate for your needs by consulting with your doctor. It is doubtful that any two doctors would agree on what to take, but differences are usually not significant. Follow your doctor's advice where it conflicts with mine. All drugs have side effects, some of which can be life threatening. All drugs can be dangerous if used incorrectly. Dosage schedules must be followed carefully.

Here's the minimum to take to the third world or a remote area: an analgesic, an antibiotic, and Oral Rehydration Solution.

Also take specific medicines you take regularly and ones you might need for complications of personal conditions, such as tobramycin eyedrops to treat infections in wearers of contact lenses.

For medications that you take regularly, bring a sufficient supply to last the entire trip. Also remember to carry at least a short supply of these on your person, in case luggage is lost or diverted. Trying to obtain specific drugs abroad can be time consuming, complicated, and at times impossible, though often costs are much lower and they can sometimes be obtained without a prescription. While there have been reports on concerns about the quality of such products, I can only think of a few instances (cardiac and seizure drugs) where this may have clinical relevance. When abroad, avoid pharmaceuticals, such as those containing iodochlorhydroxyquin for diarrhea, aminopyrines for pain, or chloramphenicol, an antibiotic sold in some countries but, because of significant side effects, not in the United States or Canada. *All drug doses and indications for using them should be checked with your doctor or the medical person giving you the prescriptions, before the trip.*

Have your doctor provide a signed statement on letterhead stationery regarding prescription medicines that you carry with you, for immigration and customs authorities if they question you. Have it state that these items are for personal use and not for sale. Make several copies, in case they keep one.

Drug names are a nightmare even for medical personnel. Manufacturers attempt to imprint their brand name in everyone's memory to further their sales. In parts of the United States and in most countries, different brand names for the same drug are in common use. Generic (official) drug names, however, are standardized throughout the world with very few exceptions. In Table 3, generic names are used with alternative names in parentheses (these are official names in some countries), and brand names for a few combination drugs are given in brackets. Learn to use generic names to facilitate information exchange in global travel.

All drugs should be kept out of the reach of children, who could ingest fatal quantities of most of them.

PERSONAL MEDICAL RECORD

People with chronic medical problems or who take medicines regularly should carry pertinent information with them. This includes a medical history summary prepared by their physician. Drugs should be listed by the generic name with the doses noted. Again, make several copies of this drug list. Any allergies to medicines and environmental substances should be recorded. It is important to have the nature of the allergic reaction documented to distinguish true allergies from adverse effects of drugs. Those with heart disease and everyone over fifty should carry a copy of a current electrocardiogram. People wearing glasses or contact lenses should carry their prescription and a spare pair of glasses with them. X-ray reports for certain chronic conditions might also be helpful. Your doctor should be able to abstract the pertinent data and arrange it in a compact format on letterhead stationery. Carry copies of prescriptions for medicines taken regularly. A so-called Living Will detailing instructions on what to do should you be found in an incapacitated state is also a good idea to include in your personal medical record.

Everyone with a personal physician should carry this person's address and phone number with them when they travel. The best phone number is the clinic or answering service, accessible 24 hours a day. The home phone is also helpful. Doctors are usually eager to assist long-standing patients who are traveling in any way they can.

The changing nature of clinical care in the US has resulted in a preponderance of specialist care by many different practitioners with little coordination from a family doctor or primary care provider. With people and organizations moving, keeping important information at hand is difficult. The group with the longest history of attempting this is MedicAlert, 2323 Colorado Avenue, Turlock, CA 95382, http://www.medicalert.org/. MedicAlert provides engraved bracelets. Members and providers can access 24-hour information at (888) 633-4298 or (209) 668-3333 from outside the US, fax (209) 669-2450. Providing appropriate updated information to the organization is the individual's responsibility and could become problematic if it changes often.

It is better to carry such information yourself; photocopy it with reduction to a manageable size, then laminate it to make it waterproof and relatively indestructible. Savvy travelers also copy, reduce, and laminate the first four pages of their passport, all required visas, their driver's license, International Certificate of Vaccination, tickets, and lists of important phone numbers, as well as any calling card access information. Arrange this together in a booklet, with printed proviso they are copies and not originals.

MEDICAL KIT

All travelers should carry a medical kit containing at least the following items:

- ✪ *Drugs from Table 3, if needed*
- ✪ *Adhesive bandages*
- ✪ *Adhesive tape (including a smooth-surface variety such as duct tape if blister-prone)*
- ✪ *Moleskin (felt padding with adhesive backing)*
- ✪ *Eugenol or oil of cloves for dental problems*
- ✪ *Tincture of benzoin (to help adhesive tape hold)*
- ✪ *Wound-closure strips*
- ✪ *Condoms and spermicidals (should be carried by all sexually active men and women)*
- ✪ *Clinical thermometer—low reading if you will be in cold climates, and high reading if in hot areas (see Table 1 for Fahrenheit-Celsius conversions)*
- ✪ *Water-purification materials (see the Water section in chapter 3)*
- ✪ *This book, annotated with notes from your own experiences and with emergency contact information*

Other useful items for a medical kit include:

- ✪ *Toilet paper*
- ✪ *Tampons*
- ✪ *Handkerchief*
- ✪ *Sunscreen and lip screen (Sunscreens are rated with a Sun Protection Factor (SPF) to indicate their degree of protection. Use one with an SPF of 15 or greater, especially when on the water, sand, or snow, or at high altitude. The best lip screens are still occlusive*

agents containing zinc oxide, or red veterinary petro-latum. Those with sunscreens are useful too.)

✪ *Syringes (If you travel to countries where there is a low standard of hygiene for giving injectable medi-cines or drawing blood, insure that the needles and syringes used (if not sterile and disposable) have been adequately sterilized (boiled for 20 minutes). Other-wise, carry some of your own or accept the risk. This is important for travel in Africa, Central and South America, and South Asia. In many of these places, especially in urban areas, you can now buy dispos-able sterile syringes.)*

✪ *Splints (Travelers undertaking hazardous activities in remote regions may want to take the versatile and effective SAM™ splint.)*

✪ *Catheter (Elderly men traveling far from help may want to carry a Foley Catheter in case of urinary obstruction.)*

Sources for hard-to-find supplies include:

Chinook Medical Gear, *120 Rock Point Drive, Unit C, Durango, CO 81301, (800) 766-1365, (970) 375-1241, fax (970) 375-6343, E-mail admin@chinookmed.com, Web site http://www.chinookmed.com.*

MASTA Travel Health Products, *London, 44 (0) 113 238 7575, Web site http://www.masta.org/index.asp. They carry lemon eucalyptus oil and other mosquito repellents, impreg-nated bed nets, and other products. There is a chat room for travel health on their website as well as a jet-lag calculator that presents light and activity prescriptions upon arrival in your destination and information for travelers with special needs.*

PREVENTIVE MEDICINES
FOR MALARIA AND DIARRHEA

In two cases, there is some rationale to taking medicines to prevent getting an illness during your travels. Such "pro-phylactic" measures are distinguished from taking a drug for treatment.

Malaria. Discuss with your doctor about taking preventive medicine against malaria if (1) your travels will take you to countries where this disease exists, (2) you will be there long enough, and (3) you will be in an environment where there is considerable risk of malaria-carrying mosquito bites. This is the one tropical disease that commonly affects and occasionally kills travelers who don't take the proper precautions. Statistically the risk is greatest for travelers to Solomon Islands, Papua New Guinea, and sub-Saharan Africa, but it is also significant in India and most other regions where the disease occurs. Much of the increased risk from malaria in Africa may be because travelers there spend more time outdoors than in other destinations where malaria is endemic. From 1980 to 1993, fifty-three U.S. travelers died from malaria, a small number compared to those succumbing to motor vehicle accidents and heart attacks abroad. The risk of getting malaria is related to the time spent in the malaria area and the number of mosquito bites received. Only a small proportion of mosquitos are infectious. Those travelers in an infectious area for less than a week might not take a prophylactic drug, especially if returning to good medical care.

Seek out a knowledgeable travel medicine doctor or clinic, and consult *HIFIT,* the CDC Hotline, or the Web-based resources listed earlier in this section for the current advice for your planned destination. It is necessary to tailor the prophylaxis plan for your type of travel in the malaria-endemic area to be visited. Experts differ in their recommendations, as there is no consensus of opinion. Taking measures to prevent mosquito bites is more important than the specific drug prophylaxis protocol. See the Bites section of chapter 3 for specific suggestions.

Resistance of the malaria parasite to chloroquine, once the prophylactic of choice, is now common in most of the world. Today mefloquine or atovaquone/proguanil [Malarone] is advised for prophylaxis in most resistant areas of the world. Side effects of sleep disturbance, increased dreaming, and symptoms of depression are reported with mefloquine, but these tend to resolve after a few weeks. You could begin the drug three to four weeks before departure to test it out. Individuals going to a high-risk malaria area could take a loading dose of 250 mg daily for 3 days, followed by the weekly regimen. There are more side effects in the first week, but higher blood levels are reached sooner, affording greater protection.

Individuals traveling in areas with highly chloroquine-resistant malaria (Southeast Asia, rural Philippines, Indonesia, Malaysia, and Papua New Guinea) might take doxycycline, 100 mg daily, as an alternative preventive measure to mefloquine. Doxycycline is advised for travelers to the Thai-Cambodian and Thai-Burma border areas and western Cambodia. Begin 1 to 2 days before entry to the malarial area and continue for four weeks after leaving the last such region on your itinerary.

For other patterns of drug allergy, or for travel in areas of resistant malaria, there are other preventive solutions. For Africa this could include weekly chloroquine with daily proguanil (not available in the United States—contact IAMAT, address listed earlier in this chapter, for further information). The dose of proguanil is 200 mg a day at the onset of exposure and for four weeks after. This regimen is not as effective as mefloquine. Consider "terminal prophylaxis" with primaquine after completing the last dose of post-travel prophylaxis if you have traveled at length in areas of high risk to *vivax* or *ovale* malaria and received many mosquito bites. You must not have G6PD deficiency.

An alternative philosophy for those with limited risk of encountering mosquitos would be to carry standby drugs for treatment of suspected attacks of malaria where no medical facilities are available. There is very little risk that the significant side effects of Fansidar will occur when the drug is used as a single-dose treatment. Other possibilities are to carry a treatment course of mefloquine, or chloroquine, or halofantrine, or mefloquine and Fansidar, or quinine *and* doxycycline or quinine *and* clindamycin. This course is advisable for brief travel to some parts of Africa, Central and South America, northeastern India, and southern China. Those populations at greater risk for not following malaria drug prophylaxis are younger, traveling independently, and receiving travel advice from multiple sources; if this fits you, consider the above regimen carefully. Others who might consider this regimen are those who have contraindications to taking antimalarials for prophylaxis, are traveling for many months, have difficulties taking preventive drugs regularly, or travel frequently to malarial areas for brief periods of time. See your doctor about this. For more information, see Fever in chapter 5. Specific up-to-date information regarding the malarial risks and resistance patterns in various countries should be obtained from the current issue of *Health Information for International Travel* and the CDC Hotline, or the Web-based resources listed earlier in this chapter.

Be aware that taking medicines to prevent malaria does not absolutely guarantee you won't get the disease, but it drastically reduces the chances. The measures in the Bites section of chapter 3 must also be followed.

Diarrhea. Sometimes traveler's diarrhea can be prevented by taking an antibiotic or by taking bismuth subsalicylate. This may be useful for short-time (less than two weeks) travelers such as heads of state, athletes, and honeymooners. Bismuth subsalicylate is the main ingredient in Pepto Bismol. The dose is two tablets, four times a day. This is not recommended for children, people with aspirin sensitivity, or those already taking large doses of aspirin for arthritis.

The antibiotics that work are levofloxacin (500 mg) or ciprofloxacin (500 mg) taken once a day. None should be taken for longer than two weeks. Women may find that antibiotics promote yeast infection, but some people use clotrimazole suppositories to control this and continue the medicine. Antibiotics are the least recommended preventive measure. Instead, I recommend carrying them for treatment of traveler's diarrhea as described in chapter 4. However, people with limited production of stomach acid due to achlorhydria, or removal of the stomach, might consider taking antibiotics for prevention if their travels will be brief.

STYLE OF TRAVEL AND HEALTH OF HOST POPULATION

In our era of globalization and the polarization of wealth that allows people from rich countries easy access to poor countries, consideration should be given to the impact of travel to destinations in the third world (better called the majority world) upon the peoples there. Since exploration began, we have exported more diseases to these places than new ones we have brought home to plague us. Today is no different, but another factor is affecting the health of those living in the countries to which we travel. Tourism, one of the largest industries in the world today, by its business nature results in many travelers looking for at least the comforts of home at their destination. Favorable exchange rates and trade policies result in tourists obtaining this at good value. The bulk of the big profits from touristic transactions are concentrated in a few hands, and this increases the income disparity in those countries. Nothing else affects the health of a population more than the range of income disparity, so the business of tourism worsens the health of the host population.

Please limit the adverse effects of this by using small "mom-and-pop" operations in the host country. Make your arrangements with local travel agencies or do it independently, stay in small inns, and travel locally in the traditional style. Avoid using lavish infrastructure built for tourism. Ask if your tastes are influencing demands for goods and services in the developing countries and consider how your presence is influencing young people. Limit your travel to one or two places that you get to know well. Learn about these places from other than travel guides. Learn some of the local language. Your negative impact on the health of the hosts will be lessened.

CHECKLIST OF TASKS TO DO AT HOME

- ✪ *Read this book, and take a first-aid course if necessary.*
- ✪ *Assemble medical records and health provider information.*
- ✪ *Obtain consul and embassy addresses and phone numbers.*
- ✪ *Leave a copy of medical record and itinerary with a responsible friend, and perhaps a backup copy with a family member.*
- ✪ *Obtain immunizations.*
- ✪ *Assemble a medical kit.*

- ✪ Consider travelers or evacuation insurance.
- ✪ Obtain *Health Information for International Travel* or call the CDC Hotline or Web resources for destination-specific material, or consult a knowledgeable health-care practitioner.

Table 1. Temperature Conversion

Normal temperature is 98.6°F (37°C). When reading thermometers, use the following formulas to convert Fahrenheit and Celsius temperatures: $°F = 9/5°C + 32$ or $°C = 5/9 (°F-32)$.					
Celsius	Fahrenheit	Celsius	Fahrenheit	Celsius	Fahrenheit
37.0	98.6	38.0	100.4	39.0	102.2
37.1	98.7	38.1	100.5	39.1	102.3
37.1	98.8	38.1	100.6	39.1	102.4
37.2	98.9	38.2	100.7	39.2	102.5
37.2	99.0	38.2	100.8	39.2	102.6
37.3	99.1	38.3	100.9	39.3	102.7
37.3	99.2	38.3	101.0	39.3	102.8
37.4	99.3	38.4	101.1	39.4	102.9
37.4	99.4	38.4	101.2	39.4	103.0
37.5	99.5	38.5	101.3	39.5	103.1
37.6	99.6	38.6	101.4	39.6	103.2
37.6	99.7	38.6	101.5	39.6	103.3
37.7	99.8	38.7	101.6	39.7	103.4
37.7	99.9	38.7	101.7	39.7	103.5
37.8	100.0	38.8	101.8	39.8	103.6
37.8	100.1	38.8	101.9	39.8	103.7
37.9	100.2	38.9	102.0	39.9	103.8
37.9	100.3	38.9	102.1	39.9	103.9
				40.0	104.0

Table 2. Immunizations

DISEASE	VACCINE	RECOMMENDED FOR	TIMING OF ADMINISTRATION	
	* = live	E =everyone	Primary Series	
		DI = those with diminished immune status and HIV PS=travel to areas with poor sanitation	number of doses	spacing
TETANUS DIPHTHERIA		E		as child
PERTUSSIS (Whooping cough)		under age 5		as child (under 5 years)
POLIOMYELITIS	Oral *	PS, booster for previously immunized adult		as child
	Injectable killed (enhanced potency)	PS, if previously not immunized as child	4	4–6 wks apart for first three
MEASLES MUMPS RUBELLA	Usually all three vaccines given in one injection, *	E except DI	1	as child
CHOLERA		no one	2	1 week apart
	Oral live attenuated	PS	1	
YELLOW FEVER	*	ONLY if required by a country to be visited	1	
TYPHOID FEVER	Vi, capsular injectable	PS	1	
	Oral *	PS	4	1 every other day
	Injectable killed bacterial	PS	2	1 month apart
HEPATITIS	Immune Globulin (Gamma Globulin)	PS	0.02ml/kg 0.06ml/kg	for stay less than 2 months every 5 months
	Hepatitis A vaccine	PS, if age 2 or older (if younger, give immune globulin)	2	initial dose 2 weeks before exposure, second after 6 months
	Hepatitis B vaccine	E	3	two, 1 month apart, one 5–11 months later
RABIES	Tissue culture-derived vaccine	see text	3 (in arm, not in buttock)	on days 1, 7 and 30
	Nervous tissue and duck embryo vaccines available in other countries			

	NOTES
Booster	# = unsafe in pregnancy
every 10 years	Travel to the former Soviet Union countries carries an increased risk of diphtheria for the unvaccinated
no	#
once as adult per lifetime	Rare risk of vaccine-induced polio, possibly safe in pregnancy, depends on risk of acquiring polio
a year after primary series	For those travelling to high-risk area and not previously immunized, oral vaccine may be preferable
if born after 1956, one booster	#, persons who have had the diseases are immune for life Rubella vaccine should not be given for 3 months before pregnancy
every 6 months	Not required, but some health officials may demand it for entry
every 3 years	Now available in Europe and Canada, may be released soon in the US. Consider in the case of peptic ulcers, gastrectomy, or achlorhydria; also if undertaking high-risk travel
every 10 years	#, though can be used if exposure to yellow fever is unavoidable. Available only at specific centers
every 2 years	
repeat 4 doses every 5 years	#, must be refrigerated and cannot take antibiotics or mefloquine with it
3 years	
	Receive just before departure; difficult to get in most places May be appropriate for short-term traveler who will never go again
every 10 years	Blood test can determine if you have had hepatitis A before and don't need the vaccine. Do this if you were born before 1945, lived abroad, or had a history of hepatitis
	I recommend it for most all travelers, especially for those who will be abroad for more than a year or do health care work
every 2 years (better to have antibody response tested periodically to determine need for further doses)	Expensive, does not eliminate need for further injections after being bitten. There are two dosages and routes of administration. If taking chloroquine or mefloquine, you should not use the intradermal route. Repeated booster doses should be avoided unless exposure to rabies persists and antibody levels fall.

Table 2. Immunizations *Continued*

DISEASE	VACCINE	RECOMMENDED FOR	TIMING OF ADMINISTRATION	
	* = live	E =everyone	Primary Series	
		DI = those with diminished immune status and HIV PS=travel to areas with poor sanitation	number of doses	spacing
MENINGITIS	Meningococcus	DI and see Notes	1	
JAPANESE ENCEPHALITIS		Long-term travelers and residents in certain areas of South and East Asia	3	1 week apart
PLAGUE			3	two a month apart; one 6
INFLUENZA		DI	1	usually in fall
HAEMOPHILUS B		DI and everyone under 5 yrs	1	unimmunized over 15 months of age and under 5 years
			2 to 3	beginning at 2 months of age
PNEUMOCOCCUS		DI	1	
CHICKEN POX		Those who have not had the disease or have not been vaccinated for it.	2	4 to 8 weeks apart

Booster	NOTES
	# = unsafe in pregnancy
may be required every 3 years for pilgrims to Saudi Arabia	Recommended for travelers to areas where recent outbreaks have occurred or who have no functioning spleen
every 2-3 years	Hypersensitivity reactions occur up to two weeks after doses; travelers are advised not to depart until 10 days after the last dose
	Consider if you will have frequent contact with wild rodents in South America, Africa, or Asia
every year	Recommended for those with chronic lung or heart disease and/or older than 65 years # (in first trimester of pregnancy) Children 9 years of age or under who receive the vaccine for the first time need 2 doses
	#, given as well to children over age 5 and adults without a spleen, those with sickle-cell disease, Hodgkin's disease, and immune deficiency
at 15 months	For infants
no	Recommended for those without a spleen, or with a non-functioning one, those with sickle cell disease, as well as the same patients as for influenza vaccine
no	#, not for those with diminished immune status. A blood test can determine if you have had chicken pox or been vaccinated previously and thus don't need the vaccine. Local reactions and fevers can occur.

Table 3. Drug Doses and Information

CATEGORY/DRUG	USE	TYPE OF JOURNEY			FORM
		city	remote	third world	
common name (alternate name) [BRAND NAME] *=non-prescription in the USA		c = choose one In this category x = recommended o = optional			
ANALGESIC	for pain				
aspirin * (acetylsalicylic acid)	fever, pain, inflammation	c	c	c	325 mg tablet 80 mg chewable
acetaminophen * (paracetamol, APAP)	pain, fever	c	c	c	80 mg, 325 mg tablet 80 mg/5ml 160 mg/5ml
ibuprofen (* 200 mg tablet)	pain, inflammation	c	c	c	200 mg, 400 mg, 600 mg, 800 mg tablets 100 mg/5 ml
codeine phosphate	pain, diarrhea, cough	x	x	x	30 mg tablet (soluble available)
hydrocodone 5 mg plus acetaminophen 500 mg	pain, diarrhea, cough	x	x	x	combination tablet
ANTIBIOTICS	for infection				
levofloxacin			c	c	500 mg tablet
ciprofloxacin			c	c	500 mg tablet
amoxicillin clavulanate			c	c	250 mg capsule 125 mg chewable

DOSE	HOW OFTEN	COMMON SIDE EFFECTS	NOTES
A = ADULT(>12 yr) * = do NOT use in pregnancy C = child usually per kg body wt; if not listed, not recommended			
A* = 2 tablets C = 60 mg/yr	6 hours	stomach irritation	Chewable tablets recommended for children. Best to begin with 4 tablets as the first dose. Not recommended for children with infections.
2 tablets C = 60 mg/yr or 15 mg/kg	6 hours		Do use in children with fever
A* = 200-800 mg	6 hours	less stomach irritation	Common drugs of a class noted NSAID's, others (e.g. naproxen, also without a prescription) can be used instead. Individual responses to the different drugs in this class vary.
C = 5-10 mg/kg	6-8 hours		Choose one that works for you. Has effective anti-inflammatory properties. Can be used for fever in children if acetaminophen not available.
A = 1/2 to 3 tablets C = 0.5 mg/kg/dose	6 hours soluble tablets may be dissolved	abdominal upset & pain	Often combined with aspirin or acetaminophen. Soluble tablets could be used for children. Individual beneficial responses to narcotics vary; this one is the mildest.
A = 1/2 to 3 tablets C = broken tablet as per acetaminophen	6 hours	abdominal upset & pain	Another useful multi-purpose drug containing a narcotic. I advise travelers to carry one narcotic-containing analgesic. Broken tablets could be used for severe pain in children
A* = 1/2 to 1 tablet	once daily	abdominal upset, rashes	A new drug with a broad spectrum of activity; the best single expensive choice of an antibiotic to take to remote third-world areas. This or the drug below would be the choice for treating Traveler's Diarrhea.
A* = 1 to 1 1/2 tablets	12 hours	abdominal upset, rashes	Other similar drugs in this category include ofloxacin and norfloxacin. For children, naladixic acid is available.
A = 1 capsule C = 40 mg/kg/24 hrs	8 hours	diarrhea, rash	Do not give in documented penicillin allergy. The adult dose could be doubled in serious infections.

Table 3. Drug Doses and Information *Continued*

CATEGORY/DRUG	USE	TYPE OF JOURNEY			FORM
common name		city	remote	third world	
(alternate name) [BRAND NAME] *=non-prescription in the USA		c = choose one In this category x = recommended o = optional			
ANTIBIOTICS (continued)	for infection				
cefaclor			c	c	250 mg capsule 125-250 mg/5ml
erythromycin			c	c	400 mg tablet
ethyl succinate					200 mg chewable
azithromycin			c	c	250 mg tablet
doxycycline			o	o	100 mg capsule
ORAL REHYDRATION SOLUTION	to treat dehydration				
WHO Oral Rehydration Solution (ORS)*		c	c	c	1 packet
rice-based ORS* [Ceralyte]		c	c	c	1 packet
ANTIMALARIAL	to prevent and treat malaria	SEE TEXT FOR CHOICES			
chloroquine phosphate					250 mg tablet

DOSE	HOW OFTEN	COMMON SIDE EFFECTS	NOTES
A = ADULT(>12 yr) * = do NOT use in pregnancy C = child usually per kg body wt; if not listed, not recommended			
A = 1 capsule C = 40 mg/kg/24 hrs	8 hours		10% chance of allergic reaction if penicillin-allergic. The adult dose could be doubled in serious infections. Other similar drugs include cephalexin cephradine, cefuroxime axetil, and cefadroxil. The latter two have the convenience of twice-a-day dosing.
A = 1 tablet C = 30 mg/kg/24 hrs	6 hours	stomach upset, nausea, vomiting, diarrhea	The adult dose could be doubled in serious infections Useful for those allergic to penicillin
A = 2 tablets on day 1	then 1 tablet a day for 5 days		4 tablets once could be used for presumed chlamydia STD
A* = 1 tablet; take with full glass of water and some food	24 hours	increased risk of sunburn (use a sunscreen that blocks UVA radiation)	Not recommended for treatment of infections generally, but an alternative for prevention of diarrhea and malaria. May interfere with absorption of oral contraceptives.
mix one packet in a liter of water and take it often	often	none, although for insulin-dependent diabetics, the rice-based below is preferable	The mainstay of treatment for diarrhea, available in US from Jianas Brothers, 2533 SW Blvd, Kansas City, MO 64108, (816) 421-2880, fax (816) 421-2883, or abroad
as above	often		Source: Cera Products, 9017 Mendenhall Court, Columbia MD 21045, (410) 309-1000, fax (410) 309-4000, http://www.ceraproductsinc.com. Available in a variety of flavors.
A = 4 tabs initially then 2 tablets C = 16mg/kg init. then 8 mg/kg These are TREATMENT, not prevention doses.	initial dose then half the dose in 6 hours & at 24 & 48 hours	rare stomach upset, headache, dizziness	Used for presumptive treatment of malaria, and for prevention in the few remaining countries without resistance

Table 3. Drug Doses and Information *Continued*

CATEGORY/DRUG	USE	TYPE OF JOURNEY			FORM
		city	remote	third world	
common name					
(alternate name) [BRAND NAME] *=non-prescription in the USA		c = choose one In this category x = recommended o = optional			
ANTIMALARIAL (continued)	to prevent and treat malaria	SEE TEXT FOR CHOICES			
mefloquine [Larium]	(not for those with seizures or psychiatric problems)	if chloroquine-resistant malaria present			250 mg tablet
pyrimethamine 25 mg + sulfadoxine 500 mg [Fansidar]		if chloroquine resistance present			tablet
atovaquone 250 mg/ proguanil 100 mg [Malarone]		if malaria is a possibility			250 mg/100 mg tablet (adults) 62.5 mg/25 mg tablet (children)
ANITHISTAMINE	allergic reaction				
fexofenadine	itching		c	c	60 mg tablet
chlorpheniramine *			c	c	4 mg tablet 2 mg/5 ml susp.
ANTINAUSEANT	for nausea & vomiting				
metoclopramide			c	c	10 mg tablet
promethazine			c	c	25 mg rectal suppository or oral tablet
MOTION SICKNESS	to prevent motion sickness				
meclizine *		o	o	o	25 mg tablet

DOSE	HOW OFTEN	COMMON SIDE EFFECTS	NOTES
A = ADULT(>12 yr) * = do NOT use in pregnancy C = child usually per kg body wt; if not listed, not recommended			
A = 15-25 mg/kg C = 15 mg/kg THESE ARE TREATMENT DOSAGES	single dose	stomach upset, dizziness	Emotional upset and convulsions may be seen with treatment doses. For prevention, take 1 tablet a week before entry to a malarial area and for 4 weeks after leaving it. The children's dose for prevention is 4 mg/kg. You could take it for 3-4 weeks before entering a malarious area to gauge side effects.
A* = 3 tablets C = age 9-14, 2 tabs, age 4-8, l tab, age <4, 1/2 tab	once		Used only for presumptive treatment of chloroquine-resistant malaria; not recommended for prophylaxsis
A* = 1 tablet C = 10-20 kg, 1 children's tablet; 21-30 kg, 2 children's; 31-40 kg, 3 children's; >40 kg, 1 adult tablet	every day	rare stomach upset, headache, dizziness	New drug very effective for preventing deadly falciparum malaria, having fewer side effects than mefloquine. Take with food or milk and begin 1-2 days before entering malarious area and for a week upon return.
A* = 1 tablet C = 1/2 tablet for 6-12 years	12 hours	no sedation occurs	May be less effective than the more sedating preparations; also expensive. Others in this class are cetirizine, astemizole, and loratidine.
A = 1 tablet C = 0.35mg/kg/24hr	8 hours	some drowsiness	One of many choices, but inexpensive, and less sedating than others. Diphenhydramine [Benadryl] is widely used but quite sedating.
			Hydration is the most important aspect of treatment
A* = 1 tablet	8 hours		Do not use for more than a day
A = 1-2 suppositories	8 hours	sedation	The suppository should be kept cool, the drug can be used for motion sickness, & is especially good if combined with ephedrine 25 mg by mouth
			See also the anti-nauseant promethazine.
A = 1-2 tablets	1 hour before journey	drowsiness	Useful for symptoms of vertigo not associated with motion

Table 3. Drug Doses and Information *Continued*

CATEGORY/DRUG	USE	TYPE OF JOURNEY			FORM
common name		city	remote	third world	
(alternate name) [BRAND NAME] *=non-prescription in the USA		c = choose one In this category x = recommended o = optional			
MOTION SICKNESS (continued)	to prevent motion sickness				
scopolamine (hyoscine)		o	o	o	transdermal patch
phenytoin		o	o	o	100 mg capsule
ALLERGIC REACTION		Carry if someone in the party has had a serious allergic reaction			
[ANA-KIT] [EPIPEN]	reactions				in a syringe
ANTIDIARRHEAL	diarrhea symptoms				
loperamide *		o, c	o, c	o, c	2 mg tablet
ANTIFUNGAL					
clotrimazole *			c	c	1% cream or ointment
			c	c	500 mg vag tablet
miconazole			c	c	2% cream or ointment
ALTITUDE ILLNESS					
acetazolamide	to prevent and treat symptoms of altitude illness		to altitude		250 mg tablet

DOSE	HOW OFTEN	COMMON SIDE EFFECTS	NOTES
A = ADULT(>12 yr) * = do NOT use in pregnancy C = child usually per kg body wt; if not listed, not recommended			
			See also the anti-nauseant promethazine.
A* = 1 patch behind ear	8 hours before journey, lasts 72 hours	blurred vision, dry mouth, rapid pulse, dilated pupil on one side	Wash hands after applying patch. Side effects more severe after prolonged wear. There may be a withdrawal reaction when you stop using it. Smaller doses may be Hallucinations have occurred days after stopping the patch.
A = 1 capsule C = 15 mg/kg/day	8 hours		Doesn't cause drowsiness like the antihistamines; very effective in military studies. A single dose of 200 mg may be effective. Use for longer than 24 hours requires adjustment of dose to approximately 3 capsules a day.
A = 0.3 mg C = 0.2 mg (6-12 yr), 0.15 mg (2-6 yr), 0.1 mg (<2 yr)	repeat in 10 minutes if no improvement	palpitations, dizziness, headache, restlessness	This kit also contains chlorpheniramine, an oral antihistamine, which should be taken
			Drugs are not a substitute for fluids by mouth
A = 2 tablets initially, then one after each loose stool	after each loose stool		Maximum 8 tablets in 24 hours
A, C = rub in well	12 hours		Ointment or cream for presumptive treatment of fungal skin infections (ringworm).
A = insert	once in the evening		Carry this tablet if you are a diabetic female or prone to having vaginal yeast infections.
A, C = rub in well	12 hours		As above for skin infections
A* = 1/2 to 1 tablet C = 2-5 mg/kg	treatment: every 8 hours or more prevention: twice a day or at bedtime	increased urine output tingling of fingers, metallic taste in mouth	For prevention, begin on the day of ascent and continue for 1-2 days afterward. Do not use if allergic to sulfa drugs. Can also use to treat symptoms of altitude illness. None of these drugs have been tested in children, but could be tried if desperate.

Table 3. Drug Doses and Information *Continued*

CATEGORY/DRUG	USE	TYPE OF JOURNEY			FORM
		city	remote	third world	
common name					
(alternate name) [BRAND NAME] *=non-prescription in the USA		c = choose one in this category x = recommended o = optional			
ALTITUDE ILLNESS (continued)					
dexamethasone	treat severe symptoms		to altitude		4 mg tablet
nifedipine	treat HAPE		to altitude		10 mg capsule
EMETIC					
syrup of ipecac *	causes vomiting	carry if children in party			liquid
DENTAL					
eugenol * (oil of cloves)	dental pain from cavity	o	x	x	liquid
OPHTHALMIC ANTIBIOTIC	eye infections				
tobramycin			c	c	solution
gentamicin			c	c	solution
DECONGESTANT					
oxymetazolone *	to clear stuffy noses	o	o	o	nose spray pediatric form
pseudoephedrine *	to prevent ear discomfort in flight	o	o	o	120 mg long-release tablet
MISCELLANEOUS					
melatonin *	jet lag remedy	x	x	x	0.1 to 5 mg tablet or solution
zinc gluconate *	cold remedy	x	x	x	15 mg lozenge
SEDATIVE	jet lag				
zolpidem		o	o	o	5-10 mg tablet

DOSE	HOW OFTEN	COMMON SIDE EFFECTS	NOTES
A = ADULT(>12 yr) * = do NOT use in pregnancy C = child usually per kg body wt; if not listed, not recommended			
A* = 1-2 tablets C = 0.25 mg/kg	6 hours	rarely, serious emotional problems, especially after stopping the drug	Give for at least 2 doses to treat serious symptoms of altitude illness, provided descent is underway. Consider for children only in desperate situations.
A* = 1 tablet C = 0.25 mg/kg	as needed	lightheadedness, low blood pressure	For treating High Altitude Pulmonary Edema. Can also be used for prevention in HAPE susceptibles. Consult ALTITUDE ILLNESS book. For child use only in desperate situations.
A = 30 ml (2 tbsp) C = >1 yr, 15-30 ml, 8-12 mo, 10 ml (2 tsp)	give once, repeat in 30 minutes if vomiting hasn't occurred		Give 1 or 2 glasses of water after the medicine in adults and children over 1 year, half that in children under 1 year
	4 times a day		Soak small piece of cotton with it & insert into the cavity
A, C = 1 drop in eye	6 hours		Especially advisable if you wear contact lenses and will be far from help
A, C = 1 drop in eye	6 hours		
A, C = 1 spray in each nostril for children under 2 yrs	12 hours		Do not use for more than a few doses, since rebound stuffiness will be worse than the original problem
A = 1 tablet	half an hour before flying	drowsiness, feeling anxious	Consider taking if you often have ear discomfort while flying. Not recommended for those with high blood pressure.
A = see text	see Table 4 and text	somnolence	Effective for decreasing time spent adjusting to time zone changes
A = 1 lozenge	every 2 hours while awake	metallic taste in mouth	Effective in decreasing time spent with cold symptoms
A* = 1/2 to 1 tablet	at bedtime	drowsiness	Useful for ensuring sleep at night to speed up jet lag resolution. Not to be used at altitude or taken with alcoholic beverages. There are other short-acting hypnotics too.

2

FINDING MEDICAL HELP ABROAD

As noted in chapter 1, several organizations will help you find an English-speaking doctor on your travels. If you travel primarily to large cities almost anywhere in the world, those organizations can provide important information. However, those traveling off the beaten path may find the closest doctor is a two-week walk away, and there may be no way to call for a plane or helicopter for evacuation.

Know the emergency response phone number, if such exists, in the area where you are traveling. If you are unfamiliar with the local language, carry a phrase book. Most of these have appropriate phrases for dealing with medical problems.

Evacuation. If you must evacuate a seriously ill or injured traveler from a remote area, make the person comfortable, splint the injured areas, and use whatever local means are available for transport. Such means might include a makeshift stretcher, someone's back, a horse, camel, or yak, a dugout canoe or raft, even a car, train, or plane, depending on the circumstances. Reassure the victim. Try to have a familiar person of the same sex accompany the victim to provide needed support.

If you have not availed yourself of trip medical referral services, there are many possibilities. Take the ill or injured traveler to a university medical center, preferably one that has a medical school. If you are American, Canadian, Australian, New Zealander, or British, try to get to your country's embassy or consulates, all of which give assistance to their citizens.

Once you get the sick or injured person to a medical center in a large town, the worries are not over. Standards of care are different from what you may be used to. Trying to arrange evacuation to North America may be more difficult than getting out of the bush. Many airlines have only limited evacuation facilities, and they must be paid for in advance. Sometimes they block off eight seats for the sick person and require payment for all of them. If you have contracted with a U.S.-based air ambulance service, be aware that local regulations in some countries may prevent landings of these aircraft without special authorization. Your best allies in this difficult situation may be concerned relatives back home, as well as your personal doctor, and any political influence you or they may be able to wield.

Often, appropriate options for sophisticated care, if necessary, are places such as London, Bangkok, Hong Kong, or Cape Town. Evacuation to such centers may be easy in comparison to returning home.

Finding Health Care. Speak with the doctor of your country's embassy or consulates if possible. Ask your hotel for a doctor.

Consider inquiring at offices of overseas volunteer organizations. Examples include the U.S. Peace Corps, Canadian University Students Overseas, and Australian and British Volunteers Serving Overseas. Speak with the doctors who care for the volunteers.

If you can reach family members or friends in the United States, ask them to contact the State Department Overseas Citizens' Emergency Center. You should have briefed them about this already, as noted in chapter 1. If possible, call or E-mail home and ask your family or friends to contact your personal doctor about the medical problem. Do so yourself if you can. The more people you can enlist to work for you, the better your chances of getting the care you need. Contacting people back home may be very difficult. Communication facilities in most of the world may not be of the same high standard you are used to. Placing a collect international phone call or a credit card call may be impossible in many places in the world even though they have phone service. Cash may be the only medium of exchange. Don't overlook other means of communicating. Send telegrams, telexes, letters, or messages with ongoing travelers. Attempt to arrange phone patches with ham radio operators. The global network is huge.

Ask other people for help. Consider expatriates living where you are visiting, other travelers, and the local people. In most parts of the world, strong family-oriented cultures make helping one another just part of normal behavior. Even the poorest of villagers will often go to great difficulties to assist you.

When you obtain and pay for medical care, try to leave with an itemized bill showing the services provided, so that you can be reimbursed by your insurance company if you have one. In addition, try to get copies of pertinent exams (e.g., lab tests, X-rays, electrocardiograms) and a summary of the care provided, prepared by the person in charge.

3

GENERAL PREVENTIVE HEALTH ADVICE

While structural factors, notably income distribution, are most closely associated with the health of a population, certain behavior principles should govern an individual's life until we as a people take note of the dismal health ranking of the United States in comparison to other countries and act upon this. For more information on population health, look at http://depts.washington.edu/eqhlth/. The behaviors include eschewing tobacco and illicit drugs. Alcohol consumption should be limited. Sustained, vigorous exercise of a type that gets the heart beating rapidly, the lungs breathing forcefully, and the skin sweating for 30 to 60 minutes several times a week has physical and emotional benefits. Diet should be varied and well rounded. The balance between food intake and calorie burning should result in a relatively lean body mass. Stress is an important part of the balance of life. You must not have too much, but then, again, not too little either. Finally, physically and emotionally risky behavior should be undertaken only if it does not produce harm to others and you are willing to accept the risk to yourself.

FOOD

Most problems unique to travelers result from ingesting contaminated water and food. While the chances of eating contaminated food during travels through developed countries are considerably less than in third-world countries, problems may develop there too. Often those who suffer also have sensitive stomachs back home. On the other hand, food in third-world countries can be risky to consume. Local dishes may be safer to eat than Western dishes prepared locally. The only way around this is to prepare everything yourself in a hygienic manner or to supervise its cooking. This is usually not possible for most short-term travelers. But you can minimize the risk.

Your mantra for food is: "Boil it, cook it, peel it, or forget it."

Food should be thoroughly cooked, and served hot shortly thereafter. Avoid food on which flies have settled or food that has been standing, then is reheated. Food from sealed containers or cans usually entails less risk. Fresh fruit can be considered safe only if peeled by clean hands in a sanitary manner. Cutting fruit open with a knife is probably safe. Fresh salads are risky to consume, though this may be lessened by dipping the food items in boiling water or soaking them in an iodine solution three times more concentrated than what you might use for purifying water (see next section). None of these methods is possible to order in a restaurant, so avoid fresh salads there.

Pasteurized dairy products are probably safe, if they have not been contaminated since preparation. Ice cream is usually suspect, as are cheeses made from unpasteurized milk. Dry foods are likely to be safe.

In unhygienic environments, the dishes and cutlery provided by food servers are suspect. Drying the items with a clean towel is one recourse, or you could pour boiling water over them. In the most unclean environments, consider skipping food and hoping for cleaner fare later. Always wash your hands before eating.

In spite of all this appropriate advice to minimize health risks for the traveler, the benefits of trying to adapt to another culture and get accepted by its people may sometimes outweigh the risks of eating local food in the traditional style.

WATER

In drinking water, bacteria, viruses, and single-cell parasites are waterborne infectious agents that cause diarrhea and hepatitis. Outside of North America, Europe, and selected parts of Eurasia, it is best to assume that *all* water is potentially contaminated and to take steps to make it safe to drink. Techniques for doing so consist of boiling, chemically disinfecting, and filtering.

Boiling. Boiling water for 1 minute or less, as in the preparation of tea and coffee, is adequate to kill all infectious agents. This is true even at the altitudes ascended by travelers. Pasteurization of milk occurs at lower temperatures. Water from the hot water faucet, if allowed to run for a few minutes, might be safe, a consideration where there may be no other alternative. Immersion heaters can boil water for travelers staying in hotels with electricity. Unless the water can be transferred to a sterile or uncontaminated vessel, allow it to cool in the container in which it was boiled.

Filtering. Several devices now exist to filter out many harmful organisms. All are rather bulky and expensive, and most need occasional cleaning, which may result in water contamination. Filters advertised in the United States have undergone some testing to verify the sometimes limited claims made for them. Look for one that will kill or remove all parasites, bacteria and *viruses* unless you only need one to filter out *Giardia* in areas where this is the sole contaminant. The PUR™ and Sweetwater™ (by Cascade Designs) filters are good devices, portable and effective for most organisms. Consider all the above factors before you invest in a water filter. If you use a filter with obviously contaminated water, consider passing the water through it twice for added safety. The filters you commonly see in third-world countries contain ceramic candles (called this because of their shape) that filter out only silt and other sediment; they cannot be relied upon to make water potable.

Chemical Disinfection. Elemental iodine is the best agent, added by one of several means. The period of time you need to wait after adding the iodine and before drinking the water depends on the dose added, and the turbidity and temperature of the water. Triple the time given here for cold water, and double the dose and time for cloudy water.

Iodine tablets (tetraglycine hydroperiodide). Use one tablet per quart (liter) of water. Wait 10 minutes after the tablet has dissolved before drinking. Iodine tablets are most useful for water bottles. The tablets deteriorate in opened bottles, so buy a new bottle at least every year.

Tincture of iodine (USP). Use 5 drops per quart (liter) of clear warm water or 2 drops per glass (250 ml). Wait 10 minutes. I carry tincture in an opaque plastic dropper bottle, obtained by purchasing nose spray or drops, or eyedrops, discarding the contents, and pouring in the tincture. I find tincture of iodine also useful for removing leeches and disinfecting the skin around a wound (do not put it directly into a wound).

Overseas it may be difficult to know the exact contents of a solution called tincture of iodine. In the United States or elsewhere, look for the USP designation (United States Pharmacopeia), which indicates that the product is compounded to the correct standard with 2 percent free iodine. Names of similar products that might be found overseas are given below:

Strong Iodine Solution (BP) [British Pharmacopeia] contains 10 percent free iodine. It should be used in one-fifth the dose of American tincture of iodine, that is, 1 drop per quart (liter) of clear water.

Weak Iodine Solution (BP) is used in the same dose as tincture of iodine (USP).

Lugol's Solution is not standardized and is therefore unreliable for water disinfection. However, you might be able to learn the percent concentration of free iodine present in a particular formulation and adjust the dose.

Povidone-iodine (10 percent) solution is used in a dose of 8 drops per quart (liter), waiting 15 minutes. It is also a good disinfectant for the skin around wounds and, if diluted with water, the wound itself.

Many countries have their own pharmacopeia and standards for iodine solutions and tincture. See if they are equivalent to the British or United States ones before using, or else inquire locally for efficacy. Better still, bring tincture of iodine from home; it doesn't take up much space.

Iodine solution. This is made by adding the supernatant of crystalline iodine carried in a glass bottle. This method is potentially lethal if the crystals are ingested, and there are now commercial preparations available to make this unlikely.

Alcoholic iodine solution. Most of the tinctures and solutions mentioned above contain free iodine (the active agent), and a salt of iodine that is not active but contributes to the dose of iodine ingested and adds to the taste. Those who find the taste of iodine objectionable can have a chemist or pharmacist compound a solution for them. Prepare by dissolving 2 g of iodine in 100 ml of 95 percent ethanol. Then follow the same dose guidelines as listed above for tincture of iodine (USP). It is probably wise to discard this solution and make a fresh one each year, since the alcohol will evaporate and increase the concentration of iodine, making the dose less accurate. Most people, though, will find it easier to purchase tincture of iodine than to make their own.

Iodine or activated charcoal resin in filters through which the water passes results in safe water that lacks the iodine taste. The water should probably stand for 10 to 15 minutes after filtering through those units containing iodine to allow time for the material to work. They are effective but slow and tedious to use.

Rare individuals may be allergic to iodine. These people usually have a long-lasting skin rash when taking iodine, so they should not use this chemical for water purification. Pregnant women should have no problem with these chemical methods of water treatment. Persons with thyroid disease might conceivably have problems with the iodine ingested in the chemical treatment of water as outlined above. Discuss this with your doctor. Some people drinking large quantities of iodized water in desert environments over many years have developed thyroid problems. Consider other methods in this case.

A few pinches of vitamin C powder per quart (liter) of water can be added to remove the iodine taste, after waiting the prescribed time.

All water should be purified, including that used for brushing your teeth and for making ice. Drink bottled, carbonated beverages of well-known brands instead of untreated water. Beer and wine are probably safe. It may be safer to drink from the original container than a possibly contaminated glass, providing the outside of the can or bottle is cleaned and dried first. I do not trust locally produced bottled water in most third-world countries, because in many places where it has been tested, high rates of bacterial contamination are found. Failing other options, tap water that is too hot to touch and left to cool is safer than cold tap water. If water is cloudy or murky, let it stand to clarify.

Schistosomiasis

Schistosomiasis (bilharzia) is caused by *cercariae* (the larvae of certain microscopic worms), which swim in freshwater and are spread by snails. In endemic rural areas where poor sanitation exists, the disease is avoided by not swimming, bathing, or wading in freshwater that might harbor snails. Rafters and other small-boat adventurers to rivers where the disease is prevalent are especially at risk. These areas include most of Africa, the Middle East, the Caribbean islands, tropical South America, the Philippines, Indonesia, and East Asia. Detailed information can be found in *Health Information for International Travel.*

If you must enter such water, wear hip waders. The risk is highest near midday, peaks at the shoreline, is higher with more of the body exposed for longer, and is less in the middle of the body of water. In mice studies, application of cedarwood 7.5% DEET or sandalwood oil has a protective effect. There are no data in humans, but rafters might try this: If you accidentally come into contact with contaminated freshwater, rubbing your skin well with alcohol and toweling dry reduces the risk of infection. Repeat the brisk toweling periodically. Some people carry rubber gloves if they need to immerse their hands in freshwater. In such rural areas, heating bath water to 122°F (50°C) for 5 minutes, filtering it, or treating it with iodine as for drinking water will make it safe. Letting it stand for 48 hours (the cercarial lifespan) will also make it suitable. Swimming in chlorinated pools is safe.

HYGIENE

Washing your hands after defecation is always a good idea. Frequent bathing probably helps to minimize the risks of skin infections, and often contributes to a sense of well-being that can be an important mood elevator. In third-world environments, too many skin infections and parasites can be picked up by walking barefoot to recommend it.

Worms. Travelers to areas with poor sanitation can become infected with roundworms, hookworms, whipworms, fishing worms, pinworms, and lots of other critters, many of which live in the intestines. The key is prevention. Follow the general advice about food and drinking water earlier in this chapter. Do not walk barefoot. With most of the light worm burdens that typical travelers acquire, merely preventing reinfection will result in the freeloaders dying of old age, thereby curing the victim. Some, like tapeworms, can live to be quite old, and in general, it is well to rid yourself of those parasites once you return home. Usually worms cause few symptoms and are not cause for concern on the journey.

BITES

Animals. When in an area with dangerous animals, talk to people who live there to get advice on what animals are around, their behavior, and how to avoid them. It is important to learn about the ecology of the most dangerous animals. Use binoculars to scan open terrain. Be alert, keep your head up, and anticipate. If there is an unexpected animal around and you have an escape, take it. In areas with angry dogs, carry a stick, rather than stones, for protection. With a stick you don't run out of ammunition. Cayenne pepper spray can be a useful deterrent, but might more often result in a confrontation rather than an escape. Avoid contact with bats.

Insects. To avoid being bitten by insects, wear clothing that covers the arms and legs and is sufficiently thick to prevent insect bites. Denim is probably thick enough. Light colors seem to be less attractive to mosquitos. Tuck shirts into pants and pant legs into socks, wear a mosquito netting hat, and wear boots rather than sandals.

Use of permethrin, a synthetic pyrethroid insecticide, sprayed on clothing or used as a dip, or applied to the interiors of tents or the exterior of netting, can dramatically decrease the number of bites. A 0.5 percent clothing spray survives five to ten washings and is strongly recommended for those who will be exposed to disease-carrying insects and the ticks that spread Lyme disease. The available brand is Duranon™ Tick Repellent from Coulston Products (201 Ferry St., Easton, PA 18042, (800) 445-9927. A concentrated solution, Perma-Kill™ 4 Week Tick Killer, is also available for dilution. For military use, clothing is soaked in the concentrated solution, then sealed in a plastic bag overnight to improve penetration, and air-dried horizontally on aluminum foil. The permethrin-containing preparations (shampoo NIX™ and cream Elemite™) for treating lice and scabies may also be useful when applied to the skin as repellents; although they are not officially sanctioned for this purpose by the manufacturer, they are more widely available.

Use an insect repellent over exposed skin. Those containing higher concentrations of N, N-diethyl-meta-toluamide (DEET) are the most effective, though they also cause the most skin irritation. As with almost any substance used on or in the body, there are possible serious side effects, which are more often seen in children, especially when using concentrations of greater than 50 percent. Avoid using it on abraded or injured skin, including sunburned areas. Wash it off when no longer needed. Avoid using it when pregnant and on young children. Higher concentrations last longer, but are no more effective as repellents. Expect 30 percent-plus concentrations to last 4 hours. Controlled-release products reduce absorption into the bloodstream and prolong effectiveness. There is a new controlled-release formulation available from Sawyer Products (P.O. Box 188, Safety Harbor, FL 34695, (800) 940-4464) that may limit body absorption and give prolonged repellent effect. Always reapply repellent after swimming or heavy sweating. Avoid total body applications for days or weeks. Do not use combination sun block–repellent products. To use both on your skin, if using plain DEET preparations, apply the sunblock first, and then the repellent 10 minutes later. If using a controlled-release DEET, apply it first and then the sunblock.

Clothing can be impregnated with concentrated DEET and, if stored in airtight containers when not in use, effectiveness can be prolonged to 5 days. Consider making anklets and wrist bands from old clothes and impregnating them. This lessens contact of DEET with the bare skin.

Avon Skin So Soft™ is useful for repelling no-see-ums. The combination of DEET applied on the skin and permethrin to clothing and netting gives the greatest protection. Those wishing to use natural products on the skin can get citronella or lemon eucalyptus products, which are probably safe, when used diluted, in pregnancy and on small children. See the Medical Kit section in chapter 1 for information on MASTA, a source for Mosi-guard,™ the eucalyptus product. A 10 percent citronella product lasts up to 2 hours.

Other barrier protection includes mosquito netting worn over your face and placed over your bed. Bed netting can often be purchased ready-made or sewn to order in countries where mosquitos are a health hazard. Pyrethrin-impregnated bed nets are available from MASTA and other sources. You can also impregnate your net yourself, as described above. Cotton fabrics retain the material best. When using such a net, check it for holes and also inside for insects before you go to sleep. Recognize that the use of mosquito netting at night in areas of malaria may be as important as drug prophylaxis in preventing the disease. Mosquito coils and mats are available in many destinations, and these are effective in decreasing the number of insects within confined spaces. The ones containing pyrethrins and pyrethroids are probably safe.

Sometimes you may find critters attacking you in spite of having put a net up. If they might be bedbugs, sleep with a light on and move the bed away from the walls. If you are sleeping nude, try covering yourself with a sheet. In a hotel, use air conditioning or a ceiling fan, if available, to decrease mosquito bites.

Sea Creatures. The shark is most feared of sea creatures, though attacks are very rare. They are known to have attacked between latitudes 46 degrees N and 47 degrees S. The danger is greatest during late-afternoon and nighttime feeding, and in murky, warm water as well as near waste outlets. Movement and bright, contrasty, or reflective objects are known to attract them. Avoid brightly colored swimwear or diving equipment in shark-infested waters. Swim in groups. Do not go in shark-infested waters with open wounds, and possibly not if menstruating. If you spot a shark, face it, avoid erratic behavior, and leave with slow, purposeful movements. If the shark is too close, try firm, blunt blows to the snout, eyes, or gills. The principles for prevention of barracuda bites are similar to those for sharks.

Contact with less-threatening fish and with seemingly insignificant marine invertebrates causes more problems. These include certain corals, anemones, jellyfish, cone-shells, octopuses, sea urchins, sea cucumbers, sting rays, and sea snakes. There are too many to deal with here. Know the specific ones to look out for where you are planning to go. Learn which ones specifically occur (and how to identify them) in the region you plan to visit, and make sure you are familiar with appropriate treatments. Wear protective clothing and gloves around coral.

Snakes. Most snake bites are by nonpoisonous species that nevertheless inflict terror on the victim. Avoid poisonous snake bites by not handling reptiles, especially when you are inebriated during evening hours, the most common situation regarding venomous bites in the United States. When walking in snake-infested country, wear high-top boots and don't put your hands where you can't see them. Step on top of obstructions, rather than over them. At night carry a light. If sleeping in the open, try to elevate your bed on a cot, and tuck mosquito netting in well. When putting on your footwear in the morning, check to see that a visitor has not taken up residence there. If confronted by a snake in close quarters, keep absolutely still.

Leeches. Where leeches are prevalent, systematic checks should be made regularly for these pests. Leeches can be of the land or water variety. The land variety live in tropical rain forests, usually near paths or habitation for man or animals. They either fall out of trees and land on you, or climb up onto your legs. Suspect a leech when you have any unusual skin sensation anywhere on your body. Stop and investigate. Check your boots or shoes regularly, and remove any leeches you find. Leather high-top boots or leggings make sense in heavily infested areas. The insect repellents mentioned in the Insects section above also prevent many leech encounters. They can be applied to your skin and clothes. Dibutyl phthalate is an effective leech repellent and can last over two weeks when applied to clothing. It is available only through chemical supply houses. DEET may work too. Most travelers look for the creatures and pull them off before they bite.

TRAUMA

Trauma, especially that caused by motor vehicle accidents, results in the majority of disabilities acquired by travelers in developed countries. This is even more true in third-world countries. Trauma causes more illness to travelers in foreign countries than all the exotic diseases put together. Those away on a trip may take many more risks than at home, and neglect the usual standards of safety that govern their usual behavior. If you prevent trauma and follow the advice given in this book about avoiding food-, water-, and insect-borne diseases, few problems should result.

Essential DO's and DON'Ts for **motor vehicle travel** are:

DO: *Wear a seat belt if available.*
      Obey signs and speed limits.
      Pay close attention to driving in a strange place,
      especially if on the unfamiliar other side of the road.
      Drive defensively.

DON'T: *Drink alcohol or use intoxicating substances before*
        or while driving.
        Drive while ill.
        Use a cellular or mobile phone while driving.

Browse http://www.asirt.org. You might avoid bus and jeep travel during the night and when the weather is bad. The chances of a mishap then are greater. Be prepared to leave the vehicle if the driver is behaving irresponsibly.

In an airplane there may be a statistical benefit in avoiding more serious injury in a crash if you sit in the back of a large airplane. Commercial air travel is quite safe, even in third-world countries.

When a pedestrian in a country where the traffic is on the unfamiliar other side of the road, remember to turn your head both ways to check for traffic. Also note that in many places, pedestrians do not by custom or by law have the right of way. Wear bright clothing during the day and reflective clothing at night.

Water sports also contribute to significant accidents among travelers. Follow the usual water-safety principles and especially do not dive or jump into unknown waters. Wear life jackets on small boats. Do not drink alcohol while swimming.

FLYING AND JET LAG

Modern air transportation can result in rapid changes of time zones. In the course of half a day, it is possible to be 12 hours out of phase with the normal day/night, sleep/wake cycle. Even crossing two time zones can produce disturbances in normal body rhythms. Typical symptoms of jet lag include loss of appetite, difficulty sleeping, irritability, lassitude, and a general feeling of malaise. Older people are more severely affected.

Light therapy, which suppresses melatonin secretion, is effective for jet lag and is detailed in the book *How to Beat Jet Lag: A Practical Guide for Air Travelers.* For light entrainment, try not to wear sunglasses when outdoors at the times given below, and face the sun where possible during that period. Schedule optimal light exposure as follows. When heading west over n time zones, face bright outdoor light beginning at n hours before sunset for up to 6 hours. If heading east and traversing n time zones, the regimen varies. When n is 6 or less, begin light exposure at sunrise, while if n is greater than 6, begin exposure at n–6 hours after sunrise. If you are heading east for n more than twelve time zones, treat this as a westward flight of twenty-four - n time zones.

Melatonin speeds up overcoming jet lag, but the optimum dosage and timing schedule depends on an individual's body chemistry. It can be purchased in the United States from health food stores in doses of 0.1 mg to 3 mg, and is marketed variously in other countries. I find the liquid preparations the most versatile, as you can tailor the dose exactly. One regimen is the following: Upon arrival in the new time zone take 2 mg at bedtime for several days. The optimum dose should be that to induce sleep. There is no benefit from taking it at these doses before you travel. If you are still having difficulty sleeping upon arrival, consider taking a short-acting sleeping pill in small doses, such as 5–10 mg of zolpidem at bedtime or at early awakening for several days on arrival. (For possible side effects see Table 3.) Stay awake in the arrival time zone until 10:00 P.M. local time.

The alternative regimen, developed by Dr. Alfred Lewy, is depicted in the schedule in Table 4. It is specific for time zones crossed in east or west directions to optimize entraining body rhythms and may be more effective than the above regimen. The ideal dose of melatonin taken during the day varies, but 0.5 mg is recommended to start with. If 0.5 mg makes you sleepy during the day, try a smaller dose (0.1 or 0.2 mg) that doesn't make you tired. Then repeat that dose every 2 hours for three doses, instead of the single 0.5 mg dose. Closer to bedtime at the destination, larger doses of 1 to 3 mg could be taken.

Schedule flights as follows: If you are heading east, leave early in the day; if you are heading west, leave late in the day! Try to shift your rhythms before you depart. Go to sleep later if heading west, and earlier if going east.

Long air journeys can result in blood clots in the legs because of prolonged inactivity in a cramped, dry environment. Periodically, get up and walk around, and while sitting, do isometric exercises. Drink at least two cups of non-alcoholic liquids every hour. Set your watch to the destination time right after boarding and adjust your schedule to the new time.

Avoid stressful situations for the first few days after arrival in the new time zone. If you must arrange important meetings, try to schedule them for times when you would be most alert in your originating time zone. Being physically active outdoors during the day helps.

Table 4. Jet Lag Treatment with Melatonin and Light

TIME TO TAKE MELATONIN THE DAY BEFORE & DAY OF DEPARTURE			
Time Zone Change	1 to 6 hours	7 to 9 hours	10 or more hours
travel from east to west	when you awake	when you awake	when you awake
travel from west to east	about 3 pm	about 3 pm	when you awake

TIME TO TAKE MELATONIN UPON ARRIVAL			
Time Zone Change	1 to 6 hours	7 to 9 hours	10 or more hours
travel from east to west	Day 1: when you wake up	Day 1: when you wake up	Day 1: when it is the same time at departure that you took it yesterday
	Days 2 and 3: 1 to 2 hours later than the day before	Days 2 and 3: 1 to 2 hours later than the day before	Days 2 and 3: 1 to 2 hours later than the day before
travel from west to east	Day 1: when it is the same time at departure that you took it yesterday	Day 1: when it is the same time at departure that you took it yesterday	Day 1: when it is the same time at departure that you took it yesterday
	Days 2 and 3: 1 to 2 hours earlier than the day before	Days 2 and 3: 1 to 2 hours earlier than the day before	Days 2 and 3: 1 to 2 hours earlier than the day before
Melatonin dose is 0.5 mg (see text if this makes you sleepy)			

TIME PERIODS TO BE IN AND TO AVOID BRIGHT LIGHT			
Time Zone Change	1 to 6 hours	7 to 9 hours	10 or more hours
travel from east to west	get bright light later in the day	get bright light in the middle of the day, avoid bright light later in the day	get bright light in the morning, avoid bright light the rest of the day
travel from west to east	get bright light in the morning	get bright light in the middle of the day, avoid bright light later in the day	get bright light in the middle of the day, avoid bright light later in the day

SEXUAL CONTACT AND SEXUALLY TRANSMITTED DISEASES (STDs)

Abstinence is the best form of prevention. Travelers, both male and female, frequently have casual sex abroad with a previously unknown partner. As many as half of these episodes may be unprotected by condoms, because tourists feel immune to the risk of STDs. Women often select another traveler, while men tend to find locals. Women tourists are at great risk in their destination if they have contact with local young men who have sex with local or migrant prostitutes during the off-season. Some women seek out such encounters. Male tourists often have contact with local prostitutes, when they would not at home. As the inequity of global economic forces increases income and wealth inequality, the sexual economy will present greater temptations to travelers. STDs acquired during travel include some rarely found back home. The risk of acquiring HIV increases when you have another STD. Choose low-risk partners, if any, and do not allow alcohol or other drugs to cloud judgment.

Both men and women travelers should carry condoms from home and have them conveniently accessible to use. Vaginal spermicidal foams, sponges, jellies, and tablets offer some protection for women but less than a man using a condom. In addition, investigate the situation. Ask the person if they have any sexually transmitted disease, sore, or discharge. Check for genital sores or discharges. Look for a urethral discharge by stripping the penis, running your finger along the lower side toward the tip. Wash the genitals of any prospective partner with soap and water. Urinate after intercourse.

SUBSTANCE ABUSE

In addition to the obvious health problems associated with the use of illicit drugs, numerous political problems can ensue. Arrest for carrying drugs can result in imprisonment without the usual due process present in the United States. The stories are many of travelers who carried some substance, sometimes unknowingly for others, and were apprehended. They were placed in subhuman detention for years without being able to contact friends, relatives, or legal counsel.

Many drugs of abuse are available in third-world countries for a fraction of the price paid in the United States. The strength of the preparations may be higher than what the individual is used to, resulting in more severe adverse reactions. As in the United States, the drug is often contaminated and may cause exotic illnesses in addition to the usual scourges of hepatitis and blood-borne infections, as well as the possibility of sudden death or slow death from AIDS.

STRESS AND PSYCHOLOGICAL PROBLEMS ASSOCIATED WITH TRAVEL

Major external stresses include death of a family member, divorce, children leaving home, change of job, or moving. Minor stresses can be just about anything, and vary according to the individual. Having to wait in line is a common travel example, as is having to deal with a strange language, culture, and environment. Fear of flying is common.

Major stresses can manifest themselves in a variety of illnesses or accidents. Minor stresses usually produce specific symptoms in a given individual: headache, stomach upset, back pain, neck stiffness, or diarrhea, for example. Children may exhibit developmental regression. Panic disorder or certain phobias may appear for the first time.

People often undertake pleasure trips at crucial points in their lives—when a relationship has broken off, when they have finished their education, perhaps when they have quit a job or are considering a new venture or career. Others travel to exotic locations, sometimes in arduous circumstances, because of the glamor, prestige, or status such adventure is accorded in certain circles. It is little wonder, then, that emotional problems can sometimes crop up to disable a traveler.

Often a couple have adapted their lives back home to being apart most of the time. They then undertake travel, which puts them together for 24 hours a day, and sparks can fly because they are not used to such constant contact. Others, such as the striving executive who is always in control, may find it difficult to be a follower on an organized trip. Such people may find that their preference for structured work interferes with the pleasures of travel, where one of the greatest rewards is often the unexpected. Others may find the schedule too hectic.

Travel itself is stressful. With the speed of modern-day transportation and the ability to cross and recross time zones rapidly, facing seemingly endless hassles at borders, finding accommodations and food, as well as adjusting to different cultures can sometimes mean that daily travel may be hazardous to your health, even if intended for rest and relaxation!

Persistent sleeplessness, especially after you have overcome jet lag, may be a symptom of emotional stress. Lack of appetite and associated weight loss could signal emotional problems; continuing irritability and thoughts of suicide could be other signs. Having the most difficulty with the activities or irascibility could also be signs. In addition, travelers who continually have accidents and illnesses on the journey might be expressing the stresses in their lives this way.

As with most health problems, prevention is the key. Enroll in a fearful fliers program. Individuals who undertake a journey with emotional baggage might consider doing it with some companions to share the burden. Itineraries should be reasonable, especially for the striving individual who is always on the run. Independent travelers might consider joining a group where support may be easily available. When alone, in a very foreign environment, dealing with emotional problems can be extremely difficult.

In such cases, admitting that some of the difficulties could be emotional in nature is the major step. Important temporary remedies include attention to hygiene and diet. Wash, shower, shave, comb your hair, and dress in clean clothes. Wear ear plugs or avoid crowds if stimuli have been annoying. Seek out well-prepared, tasty food. If you have been doing everything yourself, hire porters, guides, or taxis. If you are living in the lap of luxury when this is not your nature, cook for yourself, wash your own clothes, or shop in the market on your own. Avoid mood-altering drugs, including alcohol. Substance use is the commonest cause of psychiatric evacuations. Consider whether some of the prescription medicines you are taking might be contributing to your poor outlook. Take a rest day.

If the culture shock of a third-world setting with its attendant poverty and hopelessness has you in despair, take steps to improve your psyche. Seek out help: another traveler, or a religious organization or individual. All of the world's religions are oriented toward spiritual well-being, so a Buddhist monk, a Hindu sadhu, an Islamic prelate, a Jewish rabbi, and a Christian minister or priest are all able to give succor. Or seek comfort in a family living where you are visiting. Households worldwide depend on nurturing relationships, and may be able to provide this for you in times of distress. In a major city with English-speaking doctors, seek help from a hospital or medical center. If there is a U.S., British, Canadian, Australian, or New Zealand consulate, ask to speak to an officer. They may at least be able to arrange for help. The offices of other countries might help, though being served in your own language seems especially important in times of emotional distress.

Among members of a group traveling together, someone may become more difficult to get along with and exhibit unusual behavior. Serious physical illness can also produce emotional changes, so attention should be paid to other symptoms. Methodically go through the possible causes. In the case of problems adapting to the environment, help the victim to see this, and to recognize his or her problem as a normal reaction to stress. Don't encourage guilt feelings by blaming the person for problems his or her activities may have caused. Calm acceptance of the behavior is necessary. Listening and touching are important adjuncts to help the person feel better. The discordant couple may have to spend time apart, or return home sooner rather than risk their relationship.

Finally, recognize that illness and the effects of trauma can have far-reaching effects beyond the specific injury or organ system involved. This can manifest itself in various emotional ways. Again, recognition is the key. You must be prepared to take the additional time for healing of the psyche as well as the body by not planning an overly strenuous schedule.

SPECIAL ENVIRONMENTS

Individuals venturing to special environments should allow themselves ample opportunity to learn about the various problems unique to such places. Accident-prone persons are advised to avoid risky activities. A few basic points can be made about some of the major challenging settings for travelers.

Cold Regions. Visitors to cold regions need to be well equipped to avoid hypothermia and frostbite. They need to take precautions to avoid dehydration, which increases the risks of cold injury. High altitude also increases the hazards.

Covering the head, getting out of the wind, drying off, and improvising clothing from plastic bags, paper, and other materials can have a profound effect. Pay attention to clothing, including footwear, headgear, and gloves. Adequate hydration and diet are important. The problem is compounded if other diseases are present or the person is taking medicines. The very old and the very young are at a greater risk, as are injured persons and tall, skinny ones.

Dry and Hot Regions. Key factors for dealing with intense heat and the desert environment are to dress properly and to cover the head with a wide-brimmed hat or an umbrella. Loose-fitting garments are appropriate. Contrary to expectations, water loss by sweating is slowed by wearing clothing. Drinking lots of fluids is mandatory. If the water supply is severely limited, keep your mouth closed, refrain from talking, and limit food and salt ingestion. During intense heat, restrict activities. If necessary, be active at night.

Acclimatization to a hot and humid environment takes a week or more, as the body adjusts to sweating more without losing more salt. An adequate intake of fluids and salt is necessary, even though you may not crave these items. Do not take supplemental salt tablets. Urine should be clear, not yellow. Avoid strenuous activity in hot, humid, sunny situations until this has occurred. In times of high humidity, strenuous activity should be curtailed, especially during midday heat. Older or very young persons are more susceptible to heat illness, as are those who overexert in the heat. Those taking drugs (including alcohol) that interfere with heat loss or sweating are at greater risk. The drugs mentioned in this book do not cause this problem. Individuals with heart disease, diabetes, certain neurological disorders, and fever are at increased risk too. Be on the lookout for heat-related illness, as described in chapter 5.

High Altitude. Altitude illness affects most people above 10,000 feet (3,000 meters); some have died from it at these altitudes. The way to prevent it is to ascend slowly. This can be difficult at times, with aircraft or vehicles taking passengers to high altitude quickly. In those circumstances, taking acetazolamide, beginning the day of ascent and continuing for 2 days afterward, can prevent some of the symptoms of this problem. I prefer to not take it en route but use it to treat symptoms as described in chapter 5. If you plan to take acetazolamide, try a tablet at bedtime to see how well you tolerate it. The prophylaxis dose for an adult is one half a 250 mg tablet twice a day. Individuals allergic to sulfa drugs should not take it. Otherwise, take a few days to reach 11,000 feet (3,350 meters) and another week to reach 18,000 feet (5,500 meters). Even at this rate, some people may be unable to go to high altitudes. Thus, every member of a party has to be vigilant to see how altitude is affecting everyone else.

Other preventive measures include maintaining an adequate fluid intake. Urine should be clear, not concentrated and yellow. A high-carbohydrate diet helps. Forced deep breathing is also beneficial. Climb high, but sleep low. That means a day's excursion to a high viewpoint is fine, provided that you return to a lower altitude to sleep. Do not take any sleeping pills (sedatives or tranquillizers) at altitude. More specific material on treating altitude illness is presented in chapter 5 and in my easily carried, small-format book *Altitude Illness: Prevention and Treatment*.

Tropical Forest. Persons who have had life-threatening reactions to bee, wasp, hornet, or fire ant stings and who plan to spend considerable time in regions where such insects may be plentiful should consider a desensitization program before leaving. To treat reactions, they should certainly carry epinephrine and have members in their group know how and when to administer it. Carrying an antihistamine is also advisable.

Sea. Large ships usually have good facilities and resources for the traveler. Those concerned about sanitary conditions on specific ships that call on U.S. ports can contact the Vessel Sanitation Program, National Center for Environmental Health, Centers for Disease Control and Prevention (CDC) 4770 Buford Highway NE, Building 101, MS-F23, Atlanta GA 30341, telephone: (770) 488-7070 or 1-800-323-2132, email: vsp@cdc.gov. The "Green Sheet," which lists results of inspections, can be obtained by Internet (http://www2.cdc.gov/nceh/vsp/VSP_RptGreenSheet.asp. Those venturing forth on smaller craft need to be well prepared. The major problem is usually motion sickness (see chapter 4).

Divers should refer to texts on hazards of the underwater environment. One important caution is to avoid air flight for 12 hours after the last dive. The major problem facing the unsuspecting snorkler is contact with marine flora and fauna (see chapter 5). Coastal regions with shellfish and red tides along polluted shores are sources of potential hazard with toxins and bacteria that can kill in hours. Learn about local hazards and respect them if you forage for food.

PEOPLE WHO NEED SPECIAL CARE

Children. Travel with children of almost any age is possible, providing you plan ahead from the child's perspective, thinking of what will stimulate them and give them joy. Today useful books help in this regard. There are some risks about travel with children that you need to be familiar with while making preparations. Note your child's resting breathing rate (how many respirations per minute) when healthy. This number is a useful indicator of possible lung infection. When this rate is elevated significantly, further care is advised, as discussed in chapter 4.

Before a major overseas trip, it is best to take shorter shakedown journeys near home to learn to deal with problems. An identification bracelet is appropriate for a small child. Exercise special care with toddlers who put everything in their mouth, especially in regions with poor sanitation. Children can rapidly get dehydrated from diarrhea, and generally have less reserves than adults. Thus treat diarrhea vigorously with fluids of the variety discussed in the diarrhea section of chapter 4.

Children can rapidly become hypothermic, so keep them dressed well in colder climates. Where it is warm, provide plenty of fluids. Youngsters are usually less tolerant of different foods than adults, so you need to be prepared to provide adequate nutrition.

If you will travel to regions where malaria is present, care must be taken to properly dose children with preventive drugs, so seek out a travel clinic for the best advice. Malaria prophylaxis must be undertaken where there is a significant risk of malaria.

Mefloquine has been used safely in infants. Children being breastfed will not get adequate amounts of a drug through breast milk. Mefloquine tablets can be crushed and mixed with some jam, or a pharmacist can put appropriate amounts in a capsule.

Keep all medicines safely out of the reach of children. In case children get into the drug supply, you should carry some syrup of ipecac to empty their stomach.

High altitude should be avoided by infants, and ascent rates should be scaled down for older children. Table 3 lists children's doses of drugs that could be used along with descent in treating desperately serious cases of altitude illness. However, children should never be found in a situation to require such measures. Keep children's faces shaded in intense sunlight, on the water and snow, and up high. Use sunscreen liberally. Avoid going barefoot.

The Disabled. There has been a significant increase in resources available for those with disabilities who wish to travel. As with pregnant travelers and children, consider how much risk the disabled traveler wants to assume. There are many other resources that deal with access and where medical care might be obtained besides those listed below:

Access Board, Suite 1000, 1331 F Street N.W., Washington, D.C. 20004-1111, (202) 272-0080 (v), (202) 272-0082 (TTY), (202) 272-0081 (fax), (800) 872-2253 (v), (800) 993-2822 (TTY), http://www.access-board.gov/

Mobility International USA, P.O. Box 10767, Eugene, OR 97440, (541) 343-1284 (voice/TDD), fax (541) 343-6812, publishes A World of Options: A Guide to International Educational Exchange, Community Service and Travel for Persons with Disabilities, and other books of help to disabled world travelers. It also operates the National Clearinghouse on Disability and Exchange (clearinghouse@miusa.org, http://www.miusa.org).

Society for Accessible Travel & Hospitality, 347 Fifth Avenue, Suite 610, New York, NY 11242, (212) 447-7284, fax (212) 725-8253, E-mail sathtravel@aol.com, http://www.sath.org/

Access-able Travel Source *has much useful information.*
http://www.access-able.com/

Pregnant Women. Travel should be minimized during the last month of pregnancy. Avoid activities that pose a great risk to the mother, who has a depressed immune status and has a greater risk of acquiring infections. It would seem prudent to avoid travel to areas with poor sanitation, where insects spread serious disease, or where facilities to care for obstetrical problems are not available. Some travel infections can spread to the fetus as well. The decisions should be made on the basis of the risk that the mother is willing to take. Scuba diving should not be undertaken.

Avoid travel to regions requiring yellow fever vaccination. Immunizations for travel are best obtained from an experienced travel clinic. Mefloquine to prevent malaria is probably safe during pregnancy. Chloroquine plus proguanil has a longer record of safety in pregnancy. If malaria occurs, it needs to be treated since the disease is worse than the cure. Decisions to treat other infectious diseases, especially parasitic ones for which there exist no safe drugs for use in pregnancy, need to be made on an individual basis.

The expectant mother needs to take folate supplements and receive regular blood pressure, hemoglobin, and urine tests. Those going to remote areas should carry equipment to do this. Iodination of water is probably safe. Boiling is always safe. Fluids are the mainstay of treatment for travelers' diarrhea. Treat all fevers above 102°F (38.9°C) with acetaminophen. Avoid high altitudes unless you reside there. Get an ultrasound before remote travel.

In general do not sit for long periods during travel. Get up and walk around periodically. Make trips short, especially on buses where you may not be able to get up and walk around. Of course, smoking is to be especially avoided during pregnancy because of the harm it causes to the fetus. The same is true for alcohol.

Because of airline regulations, it is usually difficult to board a commercial airplane beyond thirty-five weeks gestation without a proper note from a doctor.

Seek help for: abdominal pain, contractions, headache, leg swelling, seizures, vaginal bleeding, and suspected rupture of membranes. It is also advisable for most other problems. Wherever you are, be aware of what medical facilities are available.

Persons With Chronic Illnesses. There are no hard and fast rules to guide travel for those with chronic medical problems. Your doctor, or a specialist in your type of illness, would be the best person to advise you on problems you might encounter and suggest ways to deal with them. Doctors tend to advise against travel to places where sophisticated medical care is not readily available for those with chronic conditions. I suggest you determine how important the trip will be to your self-esteem, and balance that against the greater risks of not being able to quickly access help. Do shakedown trips close to home. Be sure to carry ample documentation of your medical problems, as discussed in chapter 1. Ask your doctor for the contact information of doctors or clinics whom he or she may know in your destination. If your doctor doesn't know of any, ask him or her to canvas colleagues.

Persons with chronic lung disease should avoid circumstances where they will have less oxygen to breathe than they are used to. High-altitude destinations are best left off the itinerary. This can also include airplanes that are unpressurized. However, for individuals with particularly severe disease, even traveling on pressurized aircraft could cause problems since the altitude inside jets can simulate an exposure to 7,500 feet (2,200 meters). The presence of heart disease does not seem to be so restrictive. It is best to discuss this with your doctor.

Diabetics, especially those dependent on insulin, need to regulate their food intake and insulin dose. Problems are created by crossing several time zones. Frequent blood sugar monitoring is the best guide to insulin dosing during this period. Food intake needs to be regular. If taking two doses of insulin a day and heading westbound across many time zones, follow the usual regimen on the day of departure, take one-third the usual morning dose 18 hours after departure, and then the usual doses the first day upon arrival. When heading east, take two-thirds the usual morning dose at the destination morning time and then the usual evening dose, supplemented with the remaining morning dose if your blood sugar is higher than customary. Do not attempt tight glucose control; it is safer to have higher sugars.

Diabetics are advised to take sufficient insulin, syringes, and testing equipment for the entire trip. They should carry some regular insulin as well as urine ketone strips to detect and treat poor control. Their kit should also include packets of sugar and an ampule of glucagon together with instructions for its use. Consider the Medicool Insulin Protector, 20460 Gramercy Place, Torrance, CA 90501, (800) 433-2469, (310) 782-2200, http://www.medicool.com/to carry your insulin in extreme environments. Of course, wearing an identification tag or bracelet to alert others to your condition is important. *The Diabetic Traveler Newsletter*, P.O. Box 8223, Stamford, CT 06905, (203) 327-5832, may be helpful.

Individuals on dialysis can travel and receive guest services abroad. The American Association of Kidney Patients, 3505 E. Frontage Road, Suite 315, Tampa, FL 33607, (800) 749-2257, E-mail info@aakp.org, http://www.aakp.org, is a patient association. For availability of dialysis while traveling, look up Global Dialysis Centers at http://www.globaldialysis.com/for a comprehensive listing and other important information.

Persons receiving chemotherapy can consider travel if their doctor can make arrangements for them to receive proper monitoring and injections on the way. You should take a full supply of any drugs you will need. The HIV infected and other immunocompromised individuals have a greater risk of acquiring infections while traveling. They should be prepared to seek medical help expeditiously and self-treat aggressively in remote areas.

People with colostomies should bring enough supplies to last them their journey. Use a large bag when flying or when driving over significant changes in altitude. Those with gastrointestinal disorders can expect to have travel aggravate their symptoms.

Individuals with significant psychiatric illness should recognize that travel stress may upset their normal functional status. They would best not travel alone. Some psychotropic medicines might not be available overseas, so adequate stocks need to be taken. Those on lithium need to be aware of the effects on blood levels of changes in salt intake, activity levels, dramatic temperature changes, and diarrhea. Lithium levels may be unobtainable, increasing the hazards of lithium intoxication. Suicidal individuals would best not travel.

Emerging Infections and Other Fears

The media are so full of reports of "killer" infections looming everywhere, plague in India, hantavirus in the Americas, SARS in China, that people may wish to stay home. To put this in perspective, the avoidable deaths in the world resulting from the structural economic effects of income inequality number in the tens to hundreds of millions annually, and the deaths from the so-called killers pall in comparison. The high socio-economic status of most travelers, in comparison to that of their hosts, mitigates against most of the so-called scourges.

Hantavirus is fairly ubiquitous, with reservoirs in several rodent families that vary from region to region. The disease in humans can be rapidly fatal. Humans acquire the disease mostly by inhaling dried urine, saliva, and feces present in rodent habitats. This can occur to travelers if camped in tents or staying in dilapidated shelters near where rodents frequent. Tents with sealed floors and mosquito netting are advised, especially if camped under trees with dead undergrowth. Better to pitch shelters in open areas. Rinse pots and pans with iodinated water if they have been left outside. Rodent-proof your food, and don't eat anything that has been nibbled by these creatures. Avoid shelters where hygiene is poor, with food and garbage strewn about, and don't stay in any that are rat- or mouse-infested. If you must stay in potentially rat-infested abandoned buildings, first open all doors and windows, make some noise, then leave the place alone for at least 30 minutes before going in, as the rodent inhabitants are usually quite shy and will hopefully leave, and air-drying will kill the virus.

TREATING LOCAL PEOPLE ON YOUR TRAVELS

It is unlikely that during your journeys through the developed world, you will be asked to treat bystanders. However, when traveling in remote regions of the third world, local people often make the assumption that any foreigner is a doctor. They ask for medicine, which is usually what they are after, rather than advice. In such circumstances, hikers often enjoy being treated with such respect, and go out of their way to help, with sincere humanitarian intent.

This effort may do more harm than good. It destroys confidence in the medical services being developed in rural areas. It is doubtful that the brief treatment dispensed by a traveler could result in a cure or significant benefit to the sufferer. The idea that a little medicine might help a sick person get to proper medical aid just does not work. My personal experience as a doctor working in the third world, and discussions with many other informed medical personnel, suggest that giving medicine to someone whom you wish to refer to a facility is almost certain to deter that person from seeking more definitive care. Circumstances may require that you give aid, for example, at the scene of an accident. Above all, be compassionate. You are responsible for the health care of guides and porters whom you may have hired for a long trip into a remote region. You should treat their problems as you would those of your other companions.

4

COMMON ILLNESSES

Travelers on their return are often asked, "Did you have fun?" and "Did you get sick?" The answers to both are usually yes. You are more likely to have one of the afflictions discussed in this chapter than the exotic diseases you read about occurring in foreign countries. Respiratory infections and diarrhea are the two commonest problems in travelers. Moreover, these illnesses cause considerable problems and discomfort. The major risk to life and limb in travel is from injury, and the usual serious hazard is from road accidents. Adventure travelers face specific risks from particular aspects of their activities and where they are carried out. Those on commercial trips usually pay for alleged security on such travel, but participants are advised to be aware of contigency plans should accidents and illness happen. Children, the elderly, and those with chronic diseases are at greater risk of other health problems.

COLDS

Upper respiratory infections (colds) are caused by a variety of viruses. Travel to a new area results in exposure to strains the body isn't used to, and colds follow. The symptoms can be a sore throat, a runny nose, a productive cough, and malaise. High fevers are more common in youngsters than in adults. Persistent high fevers in anyone signal the need to seek medical advice.

Important preventive steps include getting enough sleep, reducing stress, eating well, and not spending time in enclosed spaces with other cold sufferers. Some people espouse the preventive benefit of high doses of vitamin C. If you believe in it and follow this back home, do so in your travels.

Once you get a cold, symptomatic measures may help. These can include whatever cold remedies you use back home. If you depend on these preparations at home, be sure to bring them along. I use **zinc gluconate** tablets (15 mg), which I take every 2 hours while awake. Studies support their use in decreasing the duration of symptoms. If you cannot clear your ears, then flying is not advised. Sometimes a decongestant (see Table 3) can result in a sufficient short-term improvement to allow air travel. Persistent use can make the situation worse than when you started, however. Another technique used to clear an ear by some frequent fliers is to place a hot, wet washcloth in a cup and then place the cup over (but not totally closing off) the ear just before takeoff or landing.

In adults with disabling cold symptoms lasting more than a week, and not showing any signs of improvement, a week's course of erythromycin might help. However, antibiotics are usually of no benefit in treating a cold and could cause harm.

With infants, it is difficult to determine if a serious problem may be present. Perhaps the best way to tell is to observe the appetite and activity of the child. If he or she loses all interest in food, liquids, and play, you may have a serious problem on your hands. Seek medical advice. Gauge the breathing rate and effort while resting, and if it's elevated (above fifty per minute) or labored, seek medical attention. If the child maintains an appetite, does not have high fevers, and is able to play and relate to his or her parents, continue the journey, but be ready to seek care if the situation changes. Give acetaminophen to lower fevers greater than 102°F (38.9°C). A child under three years old with eye discharge and fever likely has an associated ear infection and should be treated as described under ear problems in chapter 5.

A child with a sore throat, fever, and swollen glands in the neck may require a course of antibiotics, but symptomatic relief with pain medicine may be just as good. Feel your child's neck glands when he or she is healthy and note their position, size, and firmness. Then you are better able to judge changes. Penicillin V would be the good antibiotic choice, especially for tonsillitis or strep throat, a common cause for this condition. If you can see that the tonsils are inflamed (red) with some whitish material on them, and the above signs (fever, swollen glands) are present, antibiotics can be given. Amoxicillin clavulanate, erythromycin, or cefaclor are satisfactory alternatives and are listed in Table 3.

Sometimes during a cold, or after, people can get symptoms of vertigo (feeling as if the room around them is moving), which can be more pronounced when they change position. Treat this with the same drugs used for motion sickness (see later in this chapter). If the condition persists, seek help.

CONSTIPATION

Constipation is possible while traveling, changing time zones, living in strange environments, adjusting to a different schedule, eating a different diet, taking narcotic medicines (such as codeine), not having the daily routine that ensures regularity back home, and just because. The key aspects of prevention are to drink plenty of fluids, and attempt to reestablish the routine that works for you back home. Give yourself adequate time and get to a toilet when you have the urge. If you are always rushing to keep up to a schedule, you may have more problems.

Dietary measures include making sure there is adequate bulk ingested. Choose whole grains, fruit, bran, and vegetables such as carrots and celery, or whatever the local counterparts are. Most third-world diets contain plenty of bulking agents, so following native food patterns will probably ensure results. Adequate activity is important. Being recumbent day and night does not help. Stop any narcotic pain medicines, including the codeine in the medical kit. It is rare that anything else needs to be done. In unusual circumstances, a laxative might be necessary, and that should be as mild as possible.

In severe cases, where no stool has passed for a week or more and the person is very uncomfortable, the material may have to be removed with a finger. Insert a gloved or plastic-covered, lubricated finger through the anus to see if hard stool is present. In that situation, remove it piece by piece.

DIARRHEA

This problem is easier to prevent than to suffer through. Follow the recommendations regarding food and water in chapter 3. Nevertheless, even the most vigilant traveler may encounter loose and frequent stools. This is because it is hard to prevent foods and what they are served on from being contaminated (often by flies) in restaurants and homes where you eat. Diarrhea is best self-treated in most travel situations, usually with antibiotics and fluids.

When you first encounter this problem, note when the diarrhea began, and whether it came on abruptly, surprising you, and was uncomfortable enough to create anxiety about getting to a toilet in time! If such a diarrhea interrupts your daily schedule, it is probably bacterial and warrants antibiotic therapy in adults. On a short trip it makes sense to treat early. The choice of antibiotic is limited to what you have or what you can buy. Resistance varies depending on the locale, but ciprofloxacin, levofloxacin, or azithromycin are usually effective. The others listed in Table 3 could be tried, but resistance is more widespread. I used to recommend trimethoprim/sulfamethoxazole (co-trimoxazole), but, except in a few countries, it is becoming less effective. Take the antibiotic until the diarrhea abates, often after one or two doses. If you had abrupt onset of diarrhea a few days ago, and got better, then get diarrhea abruptly again, it is probably a new infection and should be treated again.

Viral diarrheas are often indistinguishable from bacterial, except that they don't get better quickly after taking antibiotics. Rotten-egg burps and foul-smelling farts can accompany bacterial and viral diarrheas and do not specify *Giardia* as the cause.

Drink fluids, clear fruit juices, caffeine-free carbonated beverages (if there is any stomach upset, nausea, or vomiting associated with the problem, let the soft drink stand until flat), and plain potable water. Get fruit juice from cans or prepare it yourself from fresh fruit or from flavored drink powder mixed with properly treated or boiled water. Frozen juices (Popsicles™), if known to be safely prepared, are a good way of getting fluids into children. Weak tea is good too, especially with some sugar. The oral rehydration fluids, especially Oral Rehydration Solution (ORS) recommended by the World

Health Organization, are best. Although ORS is not especially tasty, travelers report feeling better after consuming this solution, compared to the other choices, even in the absence of significant dehydration. In many third-world countries it can be purchased in powder packets to be made fresh. Several products available in the United States are listed in Table 3. Take comfort in knowing that few travelers die of diarrhea and subsequent dehydration, unlike children in poor countries.

A good guide to how well you are doing with fluids is to check your urine. If the urine is yellow, then you need more fluids. As a minimum, you should pass two busting bladders full of urine a day, and preferably more. Your fluid intake is probably adequate if your urine is copious and clear in color.

If you don't feel like drinking large quantities or are vomiting, sip the fluids often, a small amount at a time. More important than the actual composition of the fluid is the fact that it contains water. Diarrhea and vomiting with considerable loss of fluids, and attendant weakness and dizziness with standing, suggest the need to seek medical attention quickly. In the interim, small, frequent sips of water will result in some absorption into the system.

Add an antimotility agent if the diarrhea persists. Codeine or loperamide are common choices. One of the narcotic combinations carried for pain could be used. They should not be taken if high fever, greater than 102°F (38.9°C), or bloody stool is present. Do not use them in children. The only time that I currently use them is before a long bus ride. The antibiotic and antimotility combination is the most effective in adults. ***In any case, rehydration must be continued.*** Whether you use these additional medicines depends on how badly you feel.

If diarrhea came on gradually and was less severe, beginning as just a few loose stools, yet persisted and was perhaps accompanied by fatigue and weight loss, it is very likely that a parasite is the culprit. Further diagnostic steps are necessary, usually a stool exam. Many laboratories in other countries overdiagnose intestinal parasites, so if your diarrhea persists, seek out a good lab. Failing access to that, treat with tinidazole, which is available in many third-world countries, but not in the

United States. The adult dose is 2 gm taken daily for 2 days for *Giardia,* for 3 days for *Amoeba,* so you might try it for 3 days. Alcohol must not be consumed at that time.

Travelers are much less likely to get severe dysentery, with invasive parasitic or bacterial infections that can lead to death, a scenario that is more common in native children and in adults in poor countries. People with high fevers, severe cramps, and persistent diarrhea who are not getting better should continue to hydrate and seek medical care.

Finally, do not use any medicine containing clioquinol (iodochlorhydroxyquin) or iodoquinol (diiodohydroxyquin) unless specifically indicated by a knowledgeable physician for treatment. These drugs can cause eye problems, and although not available in the United States, may still be sold in many third-world countries. Brand names include Entero-Vioform and Mexaform.

MOTION SICKNESS

Pitching buses, bumpy airplanes, and rolling boats can make a journey miserable. People who are especially sensitive to motion sickness can make a choice of many preventive medicines. A scopolamine (hyoscine) patch placed behind the ear lasts up to 72 hours and works effectively with few side effects, except in elderly people and those with glaucoma. Some people have developed psychoses, sometimes days after using the patch. Try cutting the patch in half if side effects are bothersome. Adding dextroamphetamine, 10 mg by mouth every 12 hours, is a useful adjunct to this treatment for the serious sufferer. Other choices are meclizine, phenytoin, or promethazine. Phenytoin in a dose of 15 mg per kilogram of body weight per day in 8-hour intervals for 24 hours is effective without causing sedation. A single dose of 200 mg before the journey may help. Those who suffer greatly could take phenytoin for a long voyage at doses sufficient to maintain anticonvulsant drug levels.

Other advice includes sticking to a liquid diet and resting before the trip. Board the vehicle with an empty stomach. There may be a benefit in ginger preparations, and in the Sea Band,

Acu-Band or Relief Band applied to an acupressure point at the wrist, but studies are inconclusive. That point lies between the two prominent tendons most people show when flexing the wrist about one and a half inches (two finger widths) closer to the elbow from the wrist crease. Try pressing or scratching here for a no-cost alternative. Some suggest an ear plug in the non-dominant side (opposite to the hand you write with). Seek out the place in the bus, plane, or ship that has the least motion, usually in the middle. A semi-reclined position with the head not moving is best. Breathe slowly and deeply. Look straight ahead to the horizon, rather than off to the side, and think about more pleasant affairs.

5

LESS COMMON ILLNESSES AND PROBLEMS

"We help the blind to walk, and the lame to see."
—a notice in a clinical facility underscores the need for prevention

Judgment is the most important aspect of caring for health problems. When confronted with a health problem in a strange environment, panic is a common reaction. In most cases, it is best to stop, take a deep breath, and settle down. Then analyze the problem and take appropriate steps. How serious is the problem? What needs to be done first to preserve life and prevent further injury? What needs to be done afterward? Does anything need to be done? General first-aid knowledge cannot be learned from this book, so take a course before you leave. In addition, a good doctor's most useful medicine is often reassurance. Don't neglect to reassure a sick or injured person no matter what the apparent consequences may be.

In this chapter, a symptom or organ-system approach is followed. Recognize that in many cases an exact diagnosis can't be arrived at en route. For most people, however, this method will enable you to take some initial appropriate steps in providing care. The phrase "seek medical advice" could be added to each section; however, the material presented should help you decide whether seeking expert attention is urgently needed.

Keep notes on the problems that develop, listing the symptoms and when they occurred, as well as the specific treatment:

which drug, what dose, at what time given, and any other data that comes to mind. This is beneficial for all but the most minor problems, and especially useful for those conditions that you will refer to medical help.

Little mention is made here of the need to give pain medicine when it hurts. Except for avoiding narcotics in severe head injuries when you need to monitor the person's mental status, there is no reason not to relieve pain with the medicines in Table 3. Anti-inflammatory medicines can work well for this too. For any injury in which the skin is not seriously broken, ice application, if available, is advised. Place the ice in a plastic bag and wrap it in a towel before applying.

Non-drug methods to help an injured or ill person to relax and to divert attention from the problem may benefit in controlling pain. This usually requires active participation by the treating individual. Try to allay anxiety. Talk to the person and guide his or her imagery by having him or her recall pleasurable, relaxing events. A good example is imagining water waves on the shore. Such techniques are especially useful initially with injuries, and are mentioned further in the Dislocations section of this chapter.

In many parts of the world, local treatments for illnesses are very different from what we might use at home. Travelers often are enticed to try local cures or home remedies such as consuming various herbal preparations, communicating with a spirit medium, moxibustion, acupuncture, or voodoo surgery. Use your common sense to evaluate these cures, and if it seems that no harm will come to you, go ahead and try one. But don't neglect the practical advice in this book, which reflects practices of Western (allopathic) medicine that work.

Finally, don't look for a medicine to cure all your ills. This is fraught with hazard. For example, medicines, especially antibiotics, can often upset the natural balance in the body and produce disease themselves. Unwarranted consumption of drugs increases the risk of developing allergies. Finally, overuse of antibiotics can lead to the development of resistant bacteria and the loss of effectiveness of these important, beneficial medicines.

ABDOMINAL PAIN

New foods, new schedules, and trip anxiety can all result in stomach upset. Carrying a heavy pack with a tight waistband soon after eating a big meal can easily cause distress. Discomfort is usually centered to the esophagus in the chest, or the area over the stomach just below the breastbone. The pain is typically of a burning nature, and relief is usually obtained by taking an antacid, or bland dairy products. Liquid antacids work best, up to 2 tablespoons (30 ml) every hour if necessary. Avoid the precipitating cause for future prevention.

Be concerned when the abdominal pain is severe, associated with prolonged vomiting or cramps, and accompanied by fever and inability to move about. Most people with severe problems in the abdomen would be unable to hop about on one foot. In this case, if help is far away in time or place, don't eat food, sip small quantities of clear liquids often (Oral Rehydration Solution is best), take pain medicine, and take an antibiotic if high fever is present. When vomiting is present, use promethazine rectal suppositories.

With severe abdominal pain, appendicitis can be suspected if tenderness is present in the right lower quadrant of the abdomen. It might be inflammation in the gall bladder if the tenderness is under the lower ribs to the right of the middle. If the tenderness is diffuse with a high fever and possibly delirium, perhaps typhoid fever or an infectious colitis is present. A heart attack or gynecologic problem could also be the cause of the pain. Seeking help is the important act here.

ABSCESSES AND WOUND INFECTIONS

During your travels, you may develop a painful, red, warm, swollen lump near the surface of the skin. It is likely an abscess or boil. It may begin as a pimple. Common sites include near the anus or the groin, but it can happen anywhere. Treat by applying moist heat in the form of wet compresses using towels or washcloths or by soaking the affected part in water. Treat for 15 minutes at a time, every 2 to 4 hours. If you have a fever and feel particularly ill, then taking an antibiotic is advisable. Either way, the boil should come to a head; that is, the center will become soft. If it doesn't spontaneously drain, then assist it by puncturing the center with a sterilized needle or knife. Evacuate as much pus as possible and see if you can insert a gauze wick into the crater to keep it open for a day or two.

The drainage process can be quite painful. Don't squeeze abscesses on the face. Avoid contaminating other people and items while doing this and wash your hands carefully afterward. If they recur, consider whether your diet is adequate, whether the trip is too stressful, or whether you are neglecting norms of hygiene. People with large abscesses near important body parts should probably seek medical advice and have them drained in the proper setting with appropriate pain relief.

If a wound or cut becomes infected, it can often get red streaks or develop a swelling similar to an abscess over a portion of it. If red streaks run toward the body core from an extremity, take an antibiotic. There may often be an associated swelling of a lymph node between the source of the red streaks and the trunk. Inspect the wound carefully to see if there is an abscess there that needs to be drained. Sometimes an insignificant scratch or wound can give rise to an infection. Sometimes you have not cleaned the wound adequately to remove all the foreign material. If there is an abscess in the wound and you have used wound closure strips, remove them and try to pry the edges of the wound apart to obtain drainage. In any case, moist heat as described above is the key treatment to promote inflammation and thereby bring about drainage.

If a fever or malaise is present, use of an antibiotic is advisable. Other clues to a wound infection include localized pain, warmth, swelling, redness, tenderness, and pain with movement of the area . You must decide if an abscess is present and needs to be drained. Use hot soaks and give antibiotics.

ACHES, SPRAINS, AND STRAINS

Activity levels you are not used to back home, particularly on new recreational pursuits, can result in using muscle groups and joints in ways your body is not used to. Major weight-bearing joints such as the knee and ankle are commonly sprained. A *sprain* is a tear of the ligaments that hold bones together across a joint. It results from an unnatural twist or stress to a joint. Swelling over the joint follows, typically in a well-localized area, especially in the first few hours after the injury. Carefully examine yourself with your fingers to see where the maximum tenderness is. If it is not directly over a bone and you can walk without great discomfort, a sprain is probably the injury. Treatment involves icing the affected part for at least the first 24 hours, elevating it above the heart or at least the joint closer to your heart, and applying a compression (elastic) bandage. Ice is best administered by putting ice cubes in a plastic bag, covering with a towel, and placing over the injured part. Rest is important. Avoid strenuous activity until it can be done painlessly. Wear an elastic bandage if it helps. Taking one of the analgesics or anti-inflammatories in your kit will help reduce pain.

Strains result from tears of muscles, usually from overexertion. Most aches are similar. The treatment is the same as for sprains. Back pain often results from attempting to lift luggage and other items by bending over without using your knees. If sitting for a long time on a journey, try to get up and move around periodically. Again, ice applied soon after injury and for the first 24 hours is prudent. Rest and analgesics help. Once you are on your feet, care in lifting is necessary, as it should have been before the incident.

AIDS/HIV

The risk of acquiring Human Immunodeficiency Virus (HIV) has more to do with behavior than destination. Avoid casual sexual encounters to prevent acquiring this scourge. To lessen the risk of acquiring HIV from sexual contact, follow the principles in the Sexually Transmitted Diseases section of this chapter. Be aware that receptive anal intercourse with a possible transmitter of the virus carries the greatest risk of acquiring HIV; however, vaginal transmission is the primary method in Africa and other parts of the world.

HIV is not spread by nonsexual means outside of inadvertent transfusion with blood products or use of dirty intravenous needles. None of the immunization methods advocated in this book has any risk of HIV acquisition. There is a risk of acquiring HIV from receiving blood products that have not been screened. Most every country screens some blood, at least that used by major hospitals in capital cities. A theoretical risk occurs in receiving HIV-contaminated blood before the antibody test has turned positive. This is a minor risk at home as well as abroad.

If you are concerned about the status of blood transfusions and HIV risks in a country where you are traveling, inquire on arrival. The Red Cross is usually involved in blood transfusion services worldwide, so you could check at its offices and at the local embassy or consulate. If you are traveling with a group, all of you might note your blood types and HIV status and be prepared to donate for one another in case of an emergency. Extremely cautious individuals might even have blood cross matches run on the members before the trip to gauge compatibility possibilities. This would not obviate a pretransfusion cross match.

Those concerned with transmission of HIV from the use of syringes for medical injections should check to see how the equipment is sterilized. Today most places use disposable equipment that has been sterilized. Otherwise, consider carrying some sterile syringes and needles, but recognize that the chances of a traveler needing an injection are very small. This would best be accompanied by a prescription or notarized statement to help avoid challenges at immigration and customs. It is prudent to avoid injections unless absolutely necessary. Most medicines can be given orally. Be prepared to ask questions. If not satisfied with the answers, seek other advice. Finally, if you will have body parts pierced, tattoos implanted, dental work done, or acupuncture performed, check to see that the equipment has been properly sterilized.

ALLERGIC REACTIONS

Serious allergic reactions can follow bee stings or the ingestion of certain foods and medicines. A serious reaction is evident when breathing is wheezy or the throat is tight, making speech and breathing difficult, or when there is general circulatory collapse (no pulse). Hives are sometimes present, but by themselves are not usually a dangerous sign of an allergy. Sensitized individuals are urged to carry an identification bracelet, injectable epinephrine, and an antihistamine and to use them in the event of a serious reaction. Cardiopulmonary resuscitation (CPR) may have to be administered in extreme cases. Fortunately, such serious reactions are rare.

Milder reactions to a non-poisonous insect bite usually involve a red or blanched, raised rash (hives) that is usually itchy, or swelling of an arm or leg. Other allergic reactions, especially to drugs, frequently produce red, generalized rashes. They may occur in people taking medicines they haven't had before. Stopping the particular agent usually results in clearing of the rash in several days, sometimes a week or more. An antihistamine can help the itchiness.

ALTITUDE ILLNESS

Preventing altitude illness is discussed in chapter 3. Here we deal with the actual manifestations of the disorder itself.

I classify altitude illness as mild or severe. Signs of mild altitude illness include headache, nausea, loss of appetite, mild shortness of breath with exertion, sleep disturbance, breathing irregularity (usually during sleep), dizziness or lightheadedness, mild weakness, and slight swelling of hands and face.

Signs of severe altitude illness include the above plus marked shortness of breath with only slight exertion; rapid breathing after resting (twenty-five or more breaths per minute in adults); wet, bubbly breathing; severe coughing spasms that limit activity; coughing up pinkish or rust-colored sputum; rapid heart rate after resting (110 or more beats per minute); blueness of face and lips (compared with another person); low urine output (less than a pint—500 ml—daily); persistent vomiting*; severe, persistent headache*; gross fatigue or extreme lassitude*; delirium; confusion, and coma*; loss of coordination; and staggering*. (The asterisks indicate symptoms of cerebral manifestations of severe altitude illness.)

It is best to assume that *any* illness at altitude is altitude illness until proven otherwise. The best way to determine this is to go down a few thousand feet and see if you get better. The clearest symptoms of altitude illness to watch for in yourself are breathlessness at rest, resting pulse of over 110 per minute, loss of appetite, and unusual fatigue while walking. The clearest ones to watch for in others are skipping meals, exhibiting antisocial behavior, and being the last person to arrive at the destination (i.e., having difficulties with walking or activity).

If you have mild symptoms, rest until you feel well enough to continue ascent. Do not go higher if you have a headache. Mild pain medicine may help. Acetazolamide may also help the altitude adjustment process. If you are having difficulty sleeping, take a half tablet (125 mg) at dinner time. You might also try it one or two times during the day to see if it helps the other symptoms. If the symptoms are not disabling and you feel like ascending, then do so but return to the previous night's altitude to sleep. When you feel better, raise your sleeping altitude cautiously and be on the lookout for further symptoms.

If you or someone with you has any of the serious symptoms, descend immediately. A strong, healthy person should accompany the victim, helping him or her avoid exertion as much as possible. There is no other satisfactory treatment. Do not wait for a doctor, a helicopter, or a rescue party. Do not wait for morning. Oxygen should be given if available or use the hyperbaric Gamow™ bag. Often, dropping 2,000 or 3,000 feet will have miraculous results. Sometimes you won't get better till you get below the altitude at which you first noticed any symptoms of altitude illness. If the cerebral manifestations of serious altitude symptoms are present (as noted above by asterisks), and you have dexamethasone, give one tablet (4 mg) by mouth every 6 hours for at least two doses. Also give acetazolamide, and if the person has great breathing difficulties and you have nifedipine, give 10 mg under the tongue, followed by 20 mg of the long-acting preparation every 8 hours. Do not consider re-ascent without further evaluation.

BITES AND STINGS

The fundamental principles of wound care discussed in the Cuts, Scrapes, and Blisters section of this chapter apply here as well. Also, take note that any bite can become infected, so the principles in the Abscesses and Wound Infections section apply too.

Dogs, Cats, and Other Mammals. Besides the basic injury of a small animal bite, there is the threat of rabies. This disease is common in many third-world countries. There is even a risk from exposure to rabid-animal material such as dust found in bat caves. Except for this rare possibility, rabies is transmitted by animal saliva in contact with a wound or break in the skin or mucous membranes. Bites of certain animals are almost never associated with a risk of rabies. These include squirrels, guinea pigs, gerbils, chipmunks, rats, mice, and opossums. *Health Information for International Travel* lists the countries that are reported to be free of rabies. Beware of foxes in Europe; mongooses in Puerto Rico; wolves and jackals in India and Israel; and dogs in Africa, Asia, and Latin America. Rabid cats outnumber rabid dogs in the United States. Worldwide, human rabies mostly occurs from dog bites.

If you are bitten by an animal that is either proven or suspected to be rabid, the key initial step is wound care. The wound should be washed out in the first 3 hours with whatever liquid is at hand. Water, or hand soap and water, are good choices and readily available. A scrubbing action is best, and the victim will have to tolerate the discomfort in presumptive cases, if local anesthetic is unavailable. If available, a 1 or 2 percent benzalkonium chloride or cetrimide solution (a hospital skin disinfectant) to scrub is ideal. An alcohol solution can be used too. If you have no clinical solution, whiskey will do. Swabs, if available, should be used to cleanse the depths of punctures with this solution. Do not attempt to close an animal bite with wound closure strips. If far from help and there is significant tissue damage, a 4- or 5-day course of antibiotics is appropriate.

Vaccinations against rabies after a bite depend on the place where you are bitten (closer to the brain is more urgent), the country or region (in Thailand, rabies causes many human deaths a year), and your degree of concern. Consult with the consular office of the U.S. Embassy in the country you are in, or with a reputable travel clinic, for advice. There is no cure for rabies, but the post-exposure vaccinations are effective if you are bitten by a rabid animal, so it is better to err on the safer side and get the shots. If you have had the rabies vaccine, then two booster injections 3 days apart of the Human Diploid Cell Vaccine (HDCV) are necessary as soon as possible after the bite. However, if you have never had the vaccine, then you need to get the HDCV immunization (five doses over a month) started as soon as possible. In addition, another shot, Rabies Immune Globulin, needs to be given with the first dose of HDCV. Inquiring at the embassy or consulate of your country or a major Western country may help locate a source of the best vaccine if HDCV is not available. In many countries the old vaccinations requiring many injections of large volumes are still used, while others have tissue culture vaccines that are preferable.

What has been described above is the safest procedure to prevent rabies if bitten by a suspect animal. Wounds closest to the brain have the shortest incubation. Animal brains can be examined to determine if they have rabies, and vaccination can await the result of the study if it only takes a day or so. Many of these procedures cannot be done in remote settings, so don't neglect the above immunotherapy in cases of suspected rabies.

Insects and Spiders. Many diseases are spread by insect bites, especially in tropical and third-world countries. Mosquitos spread malaria, yellow fever, Japanese encephalitis, filariasis, and dengue fever. Some other insect-spread diseases include river blindness by black flies, African sleeping sickness by tsetse flies, leishmaniasis by sandflies, and Chagas' disease by reduviid bugs. Many of these, especially those caused by viruses, have no treatment, making it even more essential to avoid being bitten. For prevention of insect bites, see chapter 3.

Learn when and where disease-carrying insects are active in the area you are visiting. Usually, malaria-carrying mosquitos cause the greatest threat in early morning and late afternoon, and at night. Those transmitting Japanese encephalitis work during the dawn and dusk hours. Mosquitos transmitting yellow fever and dengue fever, by contrast, are active during the day. Avoid contact by being indoors during those times. Dengue-carrying mosquitos bite shaded areas on the back of the neck, arms, and legs. They breed in urban areas in stagnant water often in cans, old automobile tires, et cetera, so if you are staying near such places, fill these in or overturn them.

Mosquito bites themselves are usually just a nuisance, and there is little you can do about disease once a bite has occurred. Multiple bites can be extremely sore and itchy. Taking an antihistamine may help, as might the application of cool, wet compresses. Scratching them can cause skin infections.

If stung by many bees or their relatives, the chances of an allergic reaction increase. Take an antihistamine and watch for the signs and symptoms noted in the Allergic Reactions section of this chapter. Most of the serious allergic reactions occur in the first 15 minutes, and almost always within 6 hours. Meat tenderizer made into a paste with water and applied to the sting site after you have removed the stinger can often provide considerable relief by breaking down the toxin. Failing that, applying a papaya poultice might help. If available, you could try holding ice to the site.

Spiders almost all contain venom, though significant poisonings in humans are quite rare. Children are more severely affected. Spiders often cling to the bite site, making it easy to determine if you've been bitten by one. Apply ice to spider bites and immobilize the region. If you know the bite was caused by the funnel-web spider of southeastern Australia, apply a snug elastic bandage over the bite. Similarly, if bitten by the brown recluse, take dexamethasone if you have it in your kit. Black widow bites, if serious, need to be treated with antivenin, especially in children.

Humans. Human bites are potentially the most harmful of all, since they routinely get infected. For all but the most minor injuries, it is advised to clean the wound thoroughly, not to close it, and to take a 4- or 5-day course of antibiotics.

Sea Creatures. Stings from many sea creatures are treated similarly. Rinse the wound immediately with seawater. Topical alcohol is the best agent to counteract the toxin, though specific stinging creatures often have natural antidotes present nearby. Vinegar works too. Remove any cysts present in the wound after counteracting the toxin. Hydrogen peroxide may help to bubble out coral dust. Give pain medicine. Hot water poured over sea urchin stings may provide pain relief, and the spines must be removed with care lest they break off under the skin. Certain stings, including those of the sea wasp, the sting ray, and some sea snakes, will cause systemic reactions, which might need treatment similar to that for snake bites, including the administration of antivenin in the case of sea wasps and sea snakes.

Snakes. If someone is bitten by a poisonous snake, recognize that often no injection of venom occurs. Reassure the victim. If pain, weakness, tingling or numbness in the affected part, fang marks, swelling, lightheadedness, extensive bruising, or shallow breathing and coma occur, then venom was probably injected. If possible, have the snake killed for examination. Be certain that no one handles the snake directly, for even if dead, it can still poison someone. Immobilize the bitten extremity with a splint and do not elevate the bite site. Transport the victim to medical care for administration of antivenin, keeping the activity level of the victim to a minimum. If you have been bitten by a neurotoxic snake (elapid or sea snake) in Australia, New Guinea, or South Africa, apply an elastic bandage over the wound to compress it. Any other treatment is controversial. There is no evidence that a constricting band helps, but a device called the *Extractor* can be used to suck out venom, without an incision, in the first minutes after a bite of a non-neurotoxic snake in North America. This is advised if help is hours away. Do not remove the compression bandage or splint until you have reached a medical facility with antivenin. Do not, under any circumstances, pack the limb in ice.

BROKEN BONES

While X-raying an injured site is the best way to determine if a bone has been broken, useful clues are to examine the injured site soon after the event to note the area of maximum tenderness.

Sometimes a separation in the bone can be felt, and swelling and tenderness will be localized to the bone rather than over a ligament as in a sprain. Usually pain is severe and limits activity. Principles of treatment are to apply ice, elevate, splint (i.e., immobilize) the area, and seek definite diagnosis. The SAM™ splint is most versatile for injuries in various sites. Temporary splints can be improvised from many materials. Use rolled newspapers, a foam sleeping pad, bulky sweaters, or branches. Commonly fractured areas are the collar bone, wrist, elbow, ribs, ankle, and nose. In most healthy people, it takes considerable force to break a bone. However in older people, and those with chronic illnesses, it can take much less.

BURNS

Remove the affected part from the source of injury, and for small burns, apply cold, usually in the form of ice packs or immersion in ice water. Done early, this may decrease the amount of injury. However in large burns, say more than 15 percent of body area, do *not* attempt this. Cover the burned area with a clean dressing, elevate, and seek help. Give pain medicine. If help will be delayed longer than a few hours, it would be prudent to give the victim plenty of fluids to drink; the Oral Rehydration Solution for diarrhea would be best. In minor burns, after an initial period of cold therapy, put a dressing over the burn and, depending on the extent of the burn, decide whether to seek help. Painful blisters form in some superficial burns. If there is no pain at the burn site, consider whether the burn is deep, or full-thickness, and thus requires medical care. Most burns covering less than 5 percent of the body (the palm covers an area of approximately 1 percent) will heal without difficulty in healthy people, though if they cover a joint, are near eyes or genitals, are full-thickness, or are on a person who is very young (under five) or older (over fifty), they need a medical evaluation.

Any burn with a possible respiratory component should be brought to medical attention. Suspect this with burns occurring in an enclosed space. If the victim has singed nasal hairs, coughs up soot, or is having difficulty breathing, seek help.

CHEST PAINS

Chest pain may be a harbinger of heart disease. Many other causes exist, including stomach ulcers and muscle strains. The risk factors include a history of cigarette smoking, a family history of heart disease (i.e., parents, aunts, or uncles with heart attacks under age fifty), diabetes, high blood pressure, and heroin or cocaine use. People who already have had a heart attack or angina or who have the risk factors should consider chest pain as a possible symptom of a heart problem. Those with angina or a history of a heart attack should consult a doctor. Those with risk factors who develop pain under the breastbone that is severe, pressurelike, radiating to the neck or left arm, or associated with sweating or shortness of breath should urgently seek care. If asked to describe the pain, and the person places a clenched fist over the breastbone, I would consider this likely coming from the heart, though absence of this sign is of no help. Cardiac pain usually lasts up to a few days. If it has persisted unchanged a week or more with normal activity, likely it isn't related to the heart. If you suspect that the chest pain has its origins in the heart, take some pain medicine and aspirin, administer oxygen if available, and quickly get to a medical center with as little exertion as possible.

COLD INJURY, HYPOTHERMIA, AND FROSTBITE

Hypothermia is termed mild if body temperature is over 90°F (32.2°C), though people at the lower end of that range appear quite sick. Suspect hypothermia in individuals who are lethargic, lack coordination, have difficulty with the activity, and seem difficult to get along with. Initially, victims will complain of feeling cold and will be shivering. They will note difficulty with fine hand movements. Later, as their temperature drops, they may stumble. When body temperature falls lower than 90°F, victims, if still conscious, will be careless about the cold. They may not do up their clothes or wear gloves, oblivious to impending doom. Mental function is further decreased. Shivering stops.

In any cold environment, it is imperative to carry a low-reading thermometer. Common ones don't go below 94°F (34°C). Take a person's temperature if there is any suspicion of hypothermia. With mild hypothermia, the individual can warm him or herself, under supervision, providing the causative factors have been removed and the victim is not suffering from other problems that prevent this. Once hypothermia is identified, take steps to treat it immediately. If the body temperature is above 90°F, the victim can be rewarmed by many different means, and will usually survive if not allowed to cool further. The key initial step is to remove the person from the source of the heat loss. Strip wet clothing and replace with dry. If this cannot be done, at least cover the person with a waterproof layer, say a plastic bag worn as a sweater. Cover the head. Get the victim out of the wind. Once further heat loss is stopped, give warm, nourishing, nonalcoholic fluids to drink, for their beneficial calming effect. Encourage a person with mild hypothermia to actively exercise. This is the most effective way to raise body temperature. Other traditional ways to warm the person with external heat include hot water bottles, heating pads, and warm stones, especially placed around the trunk and in the armpits and groin. Get the person into a sleeping bag with a warm body.

Dealing with profound hypothermia—body temperatures below 90°F (32.2°C)—is a genuine emergency. Measure the temperature rectally if necessary. Do not allow the victim any exertion, even to get out of the environment causing the problem. Exertion can cause sudden death. Provide gentle transportation; rough treatment too can result in sudden death. Do not attempt to rapidly rewarm the individual in the field. Consider the person to be safely hibernating. Give oxygen if available and prevent further heat loss. Besides removing wet clothing and replacing with dry clothing, remove constricting garments and footwear, dry and insulate the individual, and place near a source of heat, such as a fire. Institute advanced life support if facilities and skilled personnel are available. If this cannot be done, then attempt to gradually rewarm the victim, by the means noted above. Above all, be gentle. Do not assume a body that is cold because of exposure is dead. Cold, supposed corpses have been rewarmed to active functional life. If CPR is instituted, reduce chest compression rates to somewhere between the number taught and half that, based on how cold the victim is.

Suspect frostbite in the same circumstances as hypothermia. Situations in which an extremity is wet and subject to wind, and the person is dehydrated and physically exhausted, are ready-made for the development of cold injury to a body part. High altitude, certain diseases, and drugs increase the risk. Suspect frostbite if the involved area is blanched and painful, though once the tissue freezes, the pain disappears. Then there is no feeling in the area, and often the victim will neglect the problem. However, frostbite can occur without ever feeling pain, and can be severe without loss of pain. Mild frostnip occurs to ears, nose, and cheeks. Affected parts can be rewarmed by placing them next to warm skin.

Treat significant frostbite by rapid rewarming once the individual has been evacuated to a situation in which he or she will no longer need to use the affected part. Until then, the victim can walk on the affected part, or do whatever is necessary to be evacuated. In the meantime, do not rub the part with anything, neither hands nor snow. This can present a dilemma, for the evacuation process will often result in a gradual rewarming of the frostbitten part. If this is the case, try to rapidly rewarm first by immersing the extremity in a large water bath with the temperature between 100° and 108°F (38° to 42°C). It usually takes a half hour and is very painful. Give whatever pain medicines you have beforehand. Give ibuprofen if available. Progress is seen by color change; the end point is lack of further color reversal. Then keep the individual warm, dress the rewarmed part to prevent further injury, and evacuate. Do not allow the person to smoke. Reassurance and support is key.

COUGHS

Cough at low altitudes, producing thick sputum and associated with fever, can be sign of a lung infection. In children, the rate and effort of breathing, if increased and associated with a fever, is the most reliable sign. Be especially worried if the respiratory rate is fifty or more in a small child (not a newborn, in whom such a rate may be normal). Seek out help if the problem seems serious. If medical care is not available soon, take an antibiotic. Ensuring adequate fluid intake is important. Less serious coughs accompany colds and can often continue for long periods of time. Persistent coughs with no sputum can be annoying and at times debilitating. Sometimes taking codeine or another narcotic can help suppress such a cough. A new persistent cough with production of thick, colored sputum, especially in a smoker, usually warrants a week's course of an antibiotic.

CUTS, SCRAPES, AND BLISTERS

Major wounds with significant bleeding are dealt with in chapter 6.

Most minor cuts, scrapes, and similar injuries require only careful cleansing of the wound. Significant involvement of underlying structures mandates medical attention. Foreign material should be removed whenever possible. If it can't, then medical attention should be sought. Cleaning around the wound with soap and water is a good practice. Tincture of iodine can be applied to the intact skin around a wound too, but do not put it in the wound. Povidone iodine diluted one-quarter strength with water can be left in a dirty wound for 2 minutes to help decrease infection.

Water should be poured directly in the wound if the victim will allow it. Water you have purified for drinking is best, but little harm would come from using what appears to be clean water. The physical cleansing action of pouring water over the wound is most important in any significant open injury if medical attention will be delayed. Gaping wounds should probably be closed, though it is safest in any questionable case not to close the wound. Providing wounds are thoroughly cleaned and absolutely free of any foreign material, butterfly bandages or adhesive tape can be used to hold together wound edges. With serious wounds, covering the area with a sterile dressing after adequate cleansing is preferred. If you feel a wound can be stitched at a facility nearby, soon, then it is best to seek out this care right away. The so-called golden period when a cut can be safely closed is short, certainly less than 24 hours and, depending on the circumstances, often much less. For cuts on the face, the time is considerably longer.

The victim should be put on antibiotics if the wound is large or contaminated with considerable foreign matter, if the person has a chronic illness, or if the wound is located in a high-risk area. Significant high-risk areas include the hand and foot (except for minor wounds), the shin, and over a joint. This should only be done if definitive treatment will be delayed.

For minor wounds over certain parts, such as joints, and in dirty environments, apply a dressing. But if a dressing is left unattended, it increases the chance of a wound infection. After applying a dressing, change it daily and remove it after 2 or 3 days. Change it more frequently if it becomes saturated or dirty. Keeping a wound moist under a clean dressing helps it to heal faster.

Important functions of dressings are to protect the wound from contamination and more injury, to absorb secretions, to immobilize the wound, and to apply pressure on a bleeding wound. If you expect substantial drainage, use plenty of dressing material. For lacerations over an area where there would be considerable skin motion with activity, limit that activity for several days. A bulky dressing might help in those circumstances. For a major wound over a joint, fashion a splint to immobilize the area. Secure the dressing with tape or by rolling a bandage of gauze or elastic material. Check to see that the circulation beyond the wound is adequate, that is, the limb is pink and warm. All wounds should be elevated. An injury on an extremity should be carried higher than the joint next to it closer to the trunk. If the injury is particularly painful afterward, investigate to see if the area is being elevated, and that the dressing is not too tight. If in doubt, loosen it. Check if there might be a wound infection.

The value of antibiotic ointments for cuts and scrapes lies in preventing the dressing from sticking to the wound and in keeping it moist. Their use is no substitution for thorough cleansing. One of the constituents of many brands of ointments, neomycin, often causes allergic reactions, especially when used over skin with eczema or chronic damage. Its allergenic effect on previously healthy skin is usually minimal. I do not routinely use these ointments. If the dressing sticks, it can be soaked off.

Blisters occur most commonly as a result of prolonged walking in new boots or shoes. If you feel some irritation, immediately apply some moleskin or smooth tape to spread the shear stresses over a larger area. Cover the moleskin if used with smooth tape. Prevent hot spots on your feet by wearing two pairs of socks, a thin synthetic inner and a substantial outer. Once a blister occurs, you can pop it with a sterilized (by holding it in a flame) needle, and then cover it with a sterile dressing for a day or two. Alternatively, you can build a cushion with layers of moleskin in which holes have been cut to accommodate the intact blister.

DENTAL PROBLEMS

Dental pain related to a tooth with a cavity can be helped by inserting a piece of eugenol-soaked cotton into the hole. Gum irritation is treated by gentle brushing and rinses using salt water or hydrogen peroxide, the full-strength solution diluted 1:4. A tender tooth with surrounding swelling, especially with a fever, might indicate an abscess and require antibiotics. If you have had persistent (a week or more), long-lasting (more than 30 seconds) heat or cold sensitivity or spontaneous pain in a tooth, a week's trial of antibiotics makes sense as a temporary measure. In any dental application requiring an antibiotic, the drug of choice is penicillin V. This has not been recommended for inclusion in the routine medical kit. Next best is amoxicillin clavulanate, then azithromycin, erythromycin, and cefaclor. In all cases, seek out a dentist for definitive care, as these are symptomatic measures only.

Travelers with extensive fillings or tooth restorations should avoid sticky foods such as toffee or hard foods, including firm nuts and ice. Unfortunately, small rocks may occur in rice and other grains and are often only noticed after biting down hard. If you break a tooth and the root is still in place, immediate care by a dentist might salvage the tooth. If the entire tooth with the root has been knocked out, there is hope if a dentist can be seen in a few hours. Clean the debris off the tooth and either place it in the space between the lower teeth and cheek or lower lip (making sure the tooth is not swallowed) or place it in a container with some milk. Or the tooth can be replaced in the socket. The dentist must be seen immediately for there to be any chance of salvage.

DISLOCATIONS

Joint dislocations may sometimes be difficult to differentiate from fractures. If there is compromise of blood circulation beyond the dislocation/fracture, then something needs to be done if you can't get to medical care in less than 2 hours. Determine this by feeling for pulses and noting their absence. Ankles, knees, and elbows are examples of joints where there may be vascular obstruction following a dislocation. It is less common with fingers and shoulders. The principles in reducing a dislocation are to reapply the force that produced it while pulling on the limb, and then to work the joint back into proper position. For fingers, pulling on them in their long axis is usually adequate. Jerky motions are less effective than steady traction. Reduction is painful, so use some of the techniques of verbal anesthesia mentioned below in regard to shoulders as well as pain medicine.

Shoulder dislocations are rather common. Usually the person notes pain in the shoulder and can't move it significantly. The action of winding up, forcing the arm back before letting go, as if throwing a baseball, is similar to the force dislocating a shoulder in many instances. If you examine the shoulder, comparing it to the other side of the body, the contours are different. If you hold an object with a straight edge against the outside of the humerus (upper arm bone), there seems to be more space between the edge of the shoulder and the arm bone than on the other side of the body. Check pulses, then reduce the shoulder if help is many hours away or if the pulses are absent beyond the dislocation and the limb is pale and blue. The easiest way to accomplish this is to help the person progressively relax the shoulder so that the joint reduces itself, sometimes with a little help from you. Give some pain medicine first. Place the person face down on a comfortable, elevated platform with the affected arm at the edge. Then as you talk to the person and have him or her fixate on some pleasurable, relaxing image (say the waves rolling into the shore at the beach), gradually have the person relax the shoulder muscles so the arm can hang down. Feel the muscle groups around the shoulder and guide the person to relax those that seem tight. The procedure can't be rushed; it will take 15 minutes to an hour or more, but is much less barbaric than most other reduction methods. Some gentle traction on the arm as it hangs down may sometimes help. You will know when the shoulder is reduced because there will be a sensation or *clunk* felt by the person and those around him or her. Then the person will be able to move the shoulder again. If this is the first dislocation for that shoulder, secure the person's arm to his or her side so he or she doesn't rotate the arm out for three weeks. Nonetheless, find medical help in that time.

EAR PROBLEMS

Those who suffer from recurrent ear discomfort associated with flying may benefit from taking pseudoephedrine 30 minutes before flying. See Table 3.

Ear pain associated with fever, especially in a child, suggests an ear infection. Seek confirmation by a health worker. If this will be delayed, take an antibiotic and analgesic. For children, amoxicillin clavulanate or cefaclor is best. Treating with pain medicine alone is probably adequate.

Slightly decreased hearing or a feeling of fullness in the ear can be caused when the eustachian tubes are blocked by congestion from a cold or by ear wax. Decongestant nose drops or spray might offer temporary relief for the former. Try to clear your ears by blowing or sucking with your mouth closed and nose held. Other methods are described in chapter 4, under Colds. Ear wax is best flushed out with body-temperature water, by standing in a shower with the nozzle aimed into the ear.

A yellowish discharge from an ear, especially after

swimming, suggests an outer ear infection, especially if not associated with decreased hearing. Drying out the ear is the key to treatment. A weak vinegar solution, 1 or 2 drops instilled four times a day on a cotton wick in the ear, would provide ideal treatment. For prevention be sure to dry your ears and especially shake out all liquid after water sports. Domeboro™ otic solution, applied to susceptible ears after swimming, may be prophylactic.

Blood emanating from an ear after a blow to the head (without a serious head injury), being near a loud blast, or deep-water diving is usually caused by a ruptured eardrum. Keep the ear clean, avoid contact with water, and take an analgesic if necessary. If the ear environment was particularly dirty (e.g., diving in brackish water), antibiotics for 5 days would be appropriate.

Eye Problems and Contact Lenses

Any burning or pain in the eye associated with some loss of vision or decrease in clarity of vision should be investigated. Use antibiotic ophthalmic drops in the interim. If you wear contact lenses and develop these symptoms, remove the lenses immediately and seek help. Again, use the antibiotic drops. In dusty environments, remove contact lenses and use glasses instead. Don't reinsert the lenses before the eye irritation has been clear for 2 or 3 days and the lenses have been disinfected.

If you get something embedded in the cornea (the clear part you see through), seek help and use the antibiotic drops. Sometimes foreign matter can get lodged under the eyelids. Try clearing it by pulling out the affected eyelid and sliding the other one under it as far as possible, allowing the eyelashes to act as a brush. If you see something on the white part of the eye, try to remove it with a wisp of cotton. If you fail to find something, look carefully in the cul de sac under the lower eyelid. Also try to evert the upper eyelid to search there. After removing something, it is prudent to put the antibiotic drops into the eye once.

When the predominant symptom is itchiness or constant watering or tearing, you may have an allergy. Try taking an antihistamine. If the white part of the eye becomes pink and is not too irritated or associated with any loss of vision, use the antibiotic drops for a few days. Then if it is not better, seek help. Finally, sometimes you might get an infection in a gland in the eyelid. Treat this "sty" with moist, comfortably hot compresses, or apply heat with a spoon that has been soaked in hot water. Heat should be applied for 10 minutes every 3 hours. It should then spontaneously drain. While the antibiotic drops won't cure it, they could be used in addition.

FEVER

In addition to specific treatment for the cause of the fever, take measures to lower the temperature. Give aspirin (not to children), acetaminophen, or ibuprofen, especially if the temperature is greater than 102°F (38.9°C). In a small child or infant, sponging with body-temperature water may help control fever. Meanwhile, search for causes of the problem.

Malaria is the most serious cause of fever in travelers in the tropics, and can cause death if not treated quickly. It can come on as little as 6 days after being bitten, or after many months. Fever 1 or 2 days after arrival in a malarial zone is not malaria. Most of the fevers experienced by travelers in the tropics are not due to malaria, but if the fever is accompanied by headache, chills, and general malaise, treat for malaria first. If you are taking mefloquine as a malaria suppressant, then take Fansidar as treatment (three tablets once) and continue the mefloquine for prevention. In areas of high chloroquine resistance, including Southeast Asia, rural Philippines, Indonesia, Malaysia, and Papua New Guinea, this may be inadequate. In such cases carry quinine and tetracycline for treatment of suspected malaria. The regimen is 650 mg quinine sulfate (two tablets) taken three times a day, together with 250 mg tetracycline, four times a day, for 7 days.

If you are not on malaria suppressants, then take the treatment course of Fansidar. An alternative would be to take a treatment course of both Fansidar and mefloquine. If there is no response and medical attention is not available, take a course of levofloxacin or ciprofloxacin for 10 days for presumptive treatment of typhoid fever. If bloody diarrhea accompanies the fever, this same treatment is suggested for bacillary dysentery. All this assumes medical help is unavailable. If you have tried one or two of the above remedies and are still sick, head for help quickly.

Often, fevers in the tropics, as in temperate zones, are caused by viruses for which there is no antibiotic treatment. The "flu" is a good example. Other rarer causes are not mentioned here, but it is important to try to arrive at an exact diagnosis to institute proper treatment. Antibiotics are only to be taken when help is far off.

FOOD POISONING AND TOXIC INGESTIONS

Mild food poisoning usually resolves in 24 hours even when accompanied by vomiting, diarrhea, and abdominal cramps. Maintain hydration as described in this chapter for diarrhea and vomiting.

Various fish and shellfish can cause severe illness when eaten. Sometimes contamination has occurred or toxin has been produced in the animal. Some of these problems can persist for a week or more. In addition to symptoms involving the gastrointestinal tract, neurological and other symptoms can occur. These include numbness, change in perception of temperatures, incoordination, joint aches, and, in rare cases, paralysis. Treatment is supportive, as noted above. If you have eaten a tuna or related species of dark-meat fish and the symptoms come on in 30 minutes, try to vomit if you have not already done so. The same advice is helpful if you have eaten reef fish such as barracuda, red snapper, grouper, amberjack, sea bass, surgeonfish, or moray eel and the symptoms come on 2 to 6 hours later. In most cases of severe fish poisoning, help should be sought.

If an unfortunate individual has taken an overdose of a drug or other toxic substance, try to empty the stomach if the item is not corrosive nor a hydrocarbon and it has just been ingested. Do not attempt this if the victim is unconscious. If you are carrying syrup of ipecac, use it. After the stomach is empty, give copious amounts of fluid to drink. If considerable time has elapsed (1 hour or more), getting the person to ingest some form of charcoal is best. Lacking medical charcoal, burnt toast granules could be tried. Seeking medical attention is urgently advised.

FOREIGN BODIES

Note: Choking caused by food or other foreign bodies becoming lodged in the throat is discussed in chapter 6.

It is usually preferable to remove foreign bodies under the skin, as infections often ensue when they are left in. With swallowed non-corrosive or nontoxic items, especially in children, just wait until they are spontaneously passed.

Outdoor activities provide some common examples. Fish hooks embedded in the skin can be removed by pushing them all the way through to have the point poke out through the skin. Then cut off the point and barb, and pull back the remainder. This is decidedly painful. Pretreat with pain medicine; wait an hour while scrupulously cleaning the area. Use verbal anesthesia, distracting the victim with conversation or some imaging procedure as described in the Dislocations section above. Finally, without hesitation, use a pair of needlenose pliers or other implement to push the hook through. Another technique, which may be less painful in the field, is to loop some string around the hook bend or belly, then pull sharply in the line of the shank, after angulating the barb away from the skin where it is snagged. Splinters and other items embedded in the skin call for similar ingenuity and improvisation. Apply the usual principles of wound care noted in the Cuts, Scrapes, and Blisters section above.

Insects can crawl into orifices, especially ears, and wreak havoc. Drown the visitor by pouring some nontoxic substance into the ear, followed by flushing it out. Ether, mineral oil, or alcohol is preferred.

For foreign bodies in the eye, see the Eye Problems and Contact Lenses section above.

GYNECOLOGICAL PROBLEMS

Menstrual problems can range from cessation of menstruation to heavy bleeding. If vaginal bleeding stops or becomes irregular, it can frequently be from the stress of travel. However, pregnancy is also a common cause. When associated breast tenderness, nausea, dietary changes, and mood changes have occurred, the latter is a strong possibility. If this was unplanned and termination is a consideration, it is safest to seek help soon to have this done in the first trimester.

Heavy bleeding in a pregnant woman demands prompt medical attention, as does modest bleeding if accompanied by fever, lightheadedness, pelvic cramps, or pain. If you are having profuse vaginal bleeding, but without pain or fever or the remotest chance that you could be pregnant, and you are far from any medical facility, you could try the following treatment. *Caution:* If you are pregnant, this treatment could harm the fetus. Take a birth-control pill four times a day for 5 days. Bleeding should stop in a day or so. After stopping the pills, you should have a menstrual period within a week. If you don't or if bleeding doesn't stop, then prompt attention is warranted.

Pelvic pain can have serious consequences if accompanied by fever (possibly due to an infection in the fallopian tubes) or if associated with pregnancy. This latter possibility can be easily overlooked and there could be a tubal pregnancy. Sometimes this could be associated with vaginal bleeding. A leaking tubal pregnancy is a distinct possibility if defecation is also very painful. The only treatment for a tubal pregnancy is surgical. Seek help immediately. If pain accompanied by discharge is the predominant symptom and you have had pelvic inflammatory disease (PID) or an infection in your tubes before, it may have recurred. Again, a precise diagnosis is important, but if there are no medical facilities, you could take an antibiotic. Take a single dose of ciprofloxacin or cefixime (400 mg), or azithromycin (1 gram), and take doxycycline or erythromycin for 10 to 14 days. If pelvic discomfort is accompanied by frequent and burning urination and sometimes by back pain, a urinary tract infection could be the cause. Refer to the Urinary Problems section below.

Vaginal discharge is often a sign of an infection, which is either yeast or sexually transmitted. Make sure you have not neglected to remove a tampon. If the discharge is cheesy in appearance and accompanied by itching, a yeast infection is a possibility, especially if you have recently been on antibiotics. Wearing occlusive nylon panties or pantyhose in a sweaty environment might also contribute to its development. Treatment can often be delayed, and airing the vaginal area—wearing cotton underwear or no underwear—can produce some relief. Consider using the clotrimazole vaginal tablet if you carry it. Otherwise, try plain yogurt douches or frequent applications of a tampon soaked in yogurt. Other discharges can be fishy in odor, frothy and foul smelling, or quite minimal. A gonorrhea, chlamydia, bacterial vaginosis, or trichomonas infection could be the cause, and each requires specific therapy. If the discharge persists or is accompanied by pelvic pain and fever, then treatment with an antibiotic listed in the previous paragraph could be attempted when there are no medical facilities.

HEADACHE

Headaches associated with a head injury are covered in the next section. Headaches often have fevers associated with them, so also check the Fever section above. Check someone with a headache and fever for a stiff neck. If the neck is stiff, and that individual seems very sick, meningitis is a possibility, and help should be urgently sought. If good care is not readily available, take an antibiotic. Throbbing headaches associated with nausea and bright lights suggest a migraine-type cause, especially if pressure over the head provides some relief. Use pain medicine. A person who never gets headaches and suddenly complains of one should seek attention quickly. Use of the analgesics and medicines for vomiting (see the Vomiting section below) can give symptom relief.

HEAD INJURIES

A momentary loss of consciousness from a traumatic event raises concern about a serious head injury. Evaluation every few hours afterward is mandatory. Look for confusion, drowsiness, poor coordination, or inability to perceive sensations or use an arm or leg. Any departure from normal behavior should be noted. If there is not a progressive improvement, or there is deterioration, help should be sought urgently. In any obviously serious head injury, seek help, and try to immobilize the neck in the interim. Bulky towels taped around the neck keep it from moving. It is best to transport the victim on a stiff board with his or her head taped to it.

If you have sustained a bump on the head, have not lost consciousness, yet don't feel perfectly normal, it is most unlikely that any serious problems will occur. The brain is protected by a strong container, and the injury must usually produce unconsciousness to be severe enough to threaten life.

HEAT ILLNESS

Heat exhaustion may be present when you have a rapid heart rate, lightheadedness, perhaps nausea, vomiting, and headache. This can progress to a loss of consciousness. Body temperature will be normal or not elevated above 102°F (38.9°C). If the victim cannot cooperate, determine the body temperature rectally. Treat with rest in the shade, fluids, and salt. Recovery should be rapid.

Heat stroke is more serious. The victim becomes confused and uncoordinated, and lapses into delirium and coma. The body temperature is high, 105°F (40.6°C) or higher, with a rapid pulse and rapid breathing. The skin sometimes feels hot and dry and does not sweat though at times can be covered with perspiration from the exercise that usually precedes this condition. This is a true medical emergency. Treat immediately by undressing and cooling the victim by any means available. Immerse in cool water, soak with wet clothes, and fan. Massage the limbs vigorously to promote circulation. Maintain these aggressive measures until the body temperature is below 102°F (38.9°C), and watch for a possible further rise in the first few hours afterward. Give fluids when the victim can accept them. The victim should avoid strenuous activity for the next few days. Recurrence is possible, and it would be prudent to move to cooler climates.

HEMORRHOIDS

Prevent hemorrhoids by avoiding constipation. Hemorrhoids may produce some blood on the outside of the stool, but the latter can also be a sign of serious illness and should be investigated when it occurs for the first time. Treat hemorrhoids by eating a bulky diet and drinking plenty of fluids. Taking mineral oil might lubricate the passage. If the hemorrhoids are sticking out and rather firm in consistency, treat them with warm water baths every few hours and keep off your feet as much as possible. Almost all such hemorrhoids will regress and allow more comfortable defecation. Do not take medicines with narcotics or antimotility drugs as for diarrhea, but other pain medicines are appropriate. If the anal area has localized tenderness and you feel quite sick and have a fever, you may have an abscess there that needs to be drained. Start hot sitz baths, take an antibiotic, and seek help.

HEPATITIS

The form of hepatitis most travelers get is hepatitis A, also called infectious hepatitis. Hepatitis produces the most sickness of any travel infection, and afflicts both neophyte and veteran travelers. It is spread by fecal-oral contamination, so the risk is greater in areas lacking modern, functioning sanitation facilities, but it also happens on standard tourist itineraries. Hepatitis A vaccine and good hygiene work to prevent this, but this remains the most frequently occurring vaccine-preventable disease. Other kinds of hepatitis can be spread sexually and by intravenous injections, or by unknown routes. Before a hepatitis victim becomes jaundiced, he or she will lose appetite, often lose the craving for cigarettes if a smoker, note increasing fatigue, and just feel out of sorts. A yellow complexion, often first noted on the whites of the eye, together with dark, tea-colored urine and pale-colored stools, follows. There is little to be done at this stage, except to prevent passing it on to others and to minimize the work the liver has to do. Wash your hands carefully after defecating and dispose of your stools so they won't infect others. Rest and avoid alcoholic beverages. Recovery takes at least several weeks and depends on the severity.

NOSEBLEEDS

Most nosebleeds can be stopped by holding the nose shut with the thumb and index finger over the fleshy part for 10 to 15 minutes. Then you must rest the nose for 24 hours. Do this by not blowing your nose, by not breathing through it (use your mouth), by not sneezing (prevent sneezes when you feel them coming by pressing your tongue against the top of the upper lip inside the mouth), and by not picking it. If bleeding continues and no help is available, spray oxymetazoline in your nose, emptying the whole bottle over an hour.

RASHES

The most common rashes are caused by allergies (review the Allergic Reactions section earlier in this chapter). They are usually red, often raised, and itchy. They may have some water-filled vesicles present. Rashes may occur where some object has contacted the skin, such as a watchband or jewelry, or where make-up has been applied. Plants, such as poison ivy or poison oak, are common causes, sometimes causing a rash in a few hours after contact in extremely sensitive individuals, or delayed by several days. Rashes can occur after taking a drug. Sometimes they occur over joints (at the wrists, elbows, and the backs of the knees); usually these individuals will have had this before. The treatment is to avoid the precipitating cause. Remove whatever substance is irritating the skin. If a plant caused the rash, scrub with water and soap not containing oil. Taking an antihistamine will help the itching, as will cool baths with baking soda. Applying a steroid cream (hydrocortisone or others) will relieve the symptoms too. In severe cases, especially early on, systemic cortisone drugs can achieve rapid improvement. Avoid putting products containing oils on the skin.

Localized rashes that are itchy, slightly raised, and ring-like can be caused by a fungal infection, in which case a trial with one of the ointments listed in Table 3 is warranted if treatment is far away. In third-world countries, a mite-caused scabies infection may be present. Attention to hygiene and using a local scabies lotion will likely help, especially if the rash is around the wrists and in the spaces between fingers.

If the rash is diffuse and accompanied by fever, then some infectious cause is likely. If the victim is very sick, then seek medical attention immediately. In the interim, take an antibiotic, ciprofloxacin if available. Skin infections in marine environments warrant antibiotic treatment. Read the section on Ticks and Leeches, below. Rash accompanying a high fever with very severe muscle and head pain could be dengue fever, caused by a mosquito-transmitted virus; see the Fever section above.

SEXUALLY TRANSMITTED DISEASES

Any genital sore needs to be evaluated by a medical person. Treatment for sexually transmitted diseases (STDs) in women is covered in the Gynecological Problems section above. A man with gonorrhea usually has a creamy yellow discharge that occurs within a few days of contact. Treat with a single dose of ciprofloxacin (750 mg), azithromycin (1 g), or cefixime (400 mg), followed by tetracycline or doxycycline for a week. In any case, it is necessary to treat your partner. Be evaluated for cure and for HIV, hepatitis B, and syphilis on returning to a medical facility. These may take three to six months to show up in tests.

Read the AIDS/HIV section in this chapter.

SUNBURN AND SNOWBLINDNESS

Many drugs can increase skin sensitivity to sunlight. Sunburn is treated as any other burn. Cooling helps, as does aspirin or an anti-inflammatory drug. Snowblindness is an intensely painful eye condition following prolonged exposure to sun, on a snowfield, especially at high altitudes, or on water, when not wearing protective glasses. It is uncomfortable to look at bright lights or even to open the eyes. Snowblindness is best treated by patching the eyes after administration of ophthalmic antibiotic eyedrops and resting a day or two. Otherwise, apply cool compresses alternatively to each eye and give pain medicine.

TICKS AND LEECHES

You can pull a leech off with fingers, chase it away with heat from a match or cigarette, or put a drop of iodine or alcohol on it. Sprinkling salt also works. Washing the resulting wound with soap and water is the most important step.

In tick-infested country, daily checks for embedded ticks are necessary. Read the Bites section in chapter 3. Ticks are best removed soon after discovery by grasping them with a tweezer as close to the skin and mouth parts as possible, and pulling straight back, gently but firmly, away from the direction the mouth parts entered into the skin. Increase the force gradually until it comes out, but don't squeeze its body. If you use your fingers, cover the tick so that you don't handle the tick with your bare skin. Then wash the wound well.

If a tick may have been attached for more than 24 hours and you remove the engorged tick in an area far from help, where poor hygiene might limit your seeing a rash, consider taking an antibiotic (doxycycline or amoxicillin are the best choices, or erythromycin for children with a penicillin allergy), for 3 to 5 days. Many diseases are spread by ticks, often involving fever, headache, and a rash. Lyme disease is a significant problem in the United States in the Northeast, Midwest, and Pacific Coast, but similar infections occur in Asia and Europe. Three-quarters afflicted don't remember a tick bite. The commonest feature early on is a ringlike rash with the center becoming purple or blistery over time. It lasts up to a month. There may be flulike symptoms and, over time, many other symptoms may appear. Early on, treating with doxycycline or amoxicillin for 10 to 21 days is recommended, but seek medical help.

TROPICAL DISEASES

Remember that common things happen frequently, so travelers in the tropics will more often have diarrhea, colds, and trauma than African Trypanosomiasis. This is not to say that you can't get exotic diseases, so if you suspect this, get yourself to a center that can deal with the problem. The primary tropical disease affecting tourists is malaria, with hepatitis second, followed by typhoid fever. Check out the Fever and Hepatitis sections earlier in this chapter.

URINARY PROBLEMS

Urinary infections are more common in women, especially after recent initiation of sexual activity. Prevent that type by drinking water before and urinating immediately after sexual intercourse. If you have frequent burning urination of small amounts, an infection is likely. Passing bloody urine, fever, and back pain are common symptoms. If the symptoms are mild, drinking copious amounts of fluids may in and of itself cure the problem, especially in a healthy individual. Drinking cranberry juice and taking vitamin C may hasten the process. If you wish to attempt a course of antibiotics, it is best to take standard doses for 3 to 5 days. If the symptoms are severe and the victim is unable to cope with travel, seek help, and take the antibiotic dose recommended in Table 3 for 10 days or until you can find help.

If men develop the symptoms noted above, a prostatic infection is possible. More likely a sexually transmitted disease is present; review the Sexually Transmitted Diseases section above. Prostatic infections could be treated with ciprofloxacin twice a day for a month.

Persons with kidney stones might be passing bloody urine and have severe crampy pain, usually on one side of the abdomen or back. Take pain medicine and drink copious amounts of fluids.

Older men who are having difficulties trying to urinate might have obstruction from a large prostate gland. If there is a considerable tender fullness (a full bladder) just above the pubic bone, help is urgently needed. If getting this will take longer than a few hours, taking an antibiotic is warranted, especially in someone with other medical problems. Try relaxing in a warm bath. Insert a Foley Catheter if available.

And, of course, don't urinate uphill or while facing into the wind.

VOMITING

Vomiting, if profuse or persistent or bloody, may be a sign of serious illness. Seek help. In the meantime, maintain hydration as for diarrhea. Replace the losses, volume for volume, with clear fluids. Oral Rehydration Solution (ORS) is best. This must be done taking small amounts (spoonfuls) often. Promethazine suppositories could be tried, though they only provide temporary symptomatic relief. Look for other symptoms to determine the cause and treat that.

6

LIFE-THREATENING EMERGENCIES

"If you can keep your head when all others around you are losing theirs, you are a man my son."
—If, *by Rudyard Kipling (apologies regarding gender-specificity)*

In an emergency, think first. Do not act impulsively. Take a few seconds to ponder the crisis, then decide what to do next. Prevent further injury and don't put yourself needlessly in danger.

Whether the victim is conscious or unconscious, identify yourself and appear to take charge with confidence. Comfort and reassure the victim. Quickly determine if anyone else nearby with more expertise than you should take charge. Otherwise delegate tasks, the most important of which is to get help. Anyone you ask to do anything should report back to you on progress.

As mentioned in chapter 5, keep notes on everything that happens to a seriously ill person.

CARDIOPULMONARY RESUSCITATION

There are two critical steps in cardiopulmonary resuscitation (CPR): when to do it and how to do it. You may have taken a course on the subject, seen demonstrations, or heard about it in the media. You may know that the process involves mouth-to-mouth respiration and heart compressions. It is tough for one person to do alone. It is also difficult to remember the correct timing of the two procedures as stated by the American Heart Association. Nevertheless, studies have shown that people who are familiar with the ideas do it well enough.

When to do CPR? You must determine that the person is not breathing, by clearing the airway and observing whether respirations occur. Do this by opening the mouth and pulling the jaw forward; hold the jaw from below near the ears and move it forward. Alternatively, reach inside the mouth and grasp the tongue to pull it forward between the teeth. If it is slippery, holding the tongue with a cloth is easier. Sweep inside and remove foreign material, dentures, etc. These techniques alone may result in resumption of breathing. If the tongue falling back in an unconscious victim has caused the problem, you could clip a safety pin through the tip of the tongue and pull it forward more easily. If there is a significant chance of a serious neck injury, don't wring the neck around, but it helps to extend the neck a little. Give traction by pulling the head away from the toes. If the person is still not breathing, then mouth-to-mouth respirations need to be started.

You must also determine whether the heart is beating to supply a pulse. Feel the carotid pulse in the neck, or feel the pulse in the groin. Check on yourself to locate these. If there is no pulse, then chest compressions must be performed together with mouth-to-mouth breathing. Don't despair; it never goes smoothly, not even in emergency departments with a trained staff. Continue until the person revives, skilled help arrives, you are exhausted, or there is no more hope. CPR is not effective for victims of blunt trauma, which is everything violent except a penetrating (stab or gunshot) wound to the chest.

BLEEDING

Bleeding is controlled by pressure over the wound. Use your hand and a clean pad, or just your (hopefully) clean hand. That's all. No tourniquets. Bleeding related to major trauma is covered in the next section.

MAJOR TRAUMA

"If I want the ultimate thrill, I've got to be willing to pay the ultimate price."

—the late great surfer Mark Foo

Major trauma is the "oh my god" variety. Sometimes you can hear the bleeding. The body may be twisted in a most unnatural way or appear uninjured. The victim may be thrashing about or lying still and making out-of-this-world breathing noises. It is time to take a deep breath and begin. First check the airway to see if the person is breathing. Then check for a pulse. After reading the discussion of CPR above, you should know what to do for these most vital functions. Try not to wring the neck but immobilize it as described under Head Injuries in chapter 5. Major bleeding must be stopped by applying pressure over the site. Place your hand directly over the pulsating artery or use a compress between your hand and the wound. Don't be concerned about washing your hands, though putting them in plastic bags if you have open sores is wise. Minor bleeding is stopped in the same manner, but doesn't need attention until later. With CPR instituted if necessary, major bleeding controlled, and the neck immobilized, the next step is to rapidly transport the victim to medical attention. Read the next section on shock. You've done your job. Don't worry about arms and legs at odd angles, but splint them if you have time.

SHOCK

This term is always in the first-aid literature and confuses people. The popular meaning of the term implies emotional stress, which is often present. The medical term denotes a life-threatening condition in which blood flow to vital organs is diminished. Suspect shock if the pulse seems weak and fast and the person appears pale, often perspiring. Treat the cause of the condition and administer intravenous fluids or blood to tide the body over. This kind of shock is present in cases of major trauma as well as many other serious situations. Rapid transport to a medical center is vitally important. Giving fluids by mouth is not usually successful because blood flow to the stomach is reduced and absorption doesn't occur. If the person vomits, this can compound the difficulties. You could try giving small amounts of Oral Rehydration Solution or other available fluid by mouth if the person is awake and capable of drinking.

The other field treatment is to keep the person warm and elevate the legs to increase blood flow.

COMA OR UNCONSCIOUSNESS

The key is to protect the airway so the individual can breathe. Follow the advice in the Cardiopulmonary Resuscitation section above. CPR may be necessary. Then try to determine the cause of the loss of consciousness. Common causes are intoxication, the state following an epileptic seizure, head trauma, heat stroke, a very severe vascular stroke, fainting, or shock following blood loss from any cause. In a diabetic, an insulin reaction must be considered. The only one of these conditions that is minor is a faint. Then the person is usually wet with sweat. Elevate the person's legs and he or she should recover in a minute or so. In the other situations, you have to treat the cause. If you suspect head trauma, protect the neck from movement. Otherwise, transport the person on his or her side, with the head somewhat lower than the rest of the body, in case he or she should vomit. Do not try to give anything by mouth to an unconscious individual. If you suspect diabetes, and glucagon is available, give an injection of one ampule under the skin. For a diabetic with any changes in mental status who is not unconscious, get them to swallow some sweet solution. In any case, seek help.

ANIMAL CONFRONTATION

Although most travelers, even those on safari, are unlikely to confront a dangerous nonhuman beast in a hostile situation, certain measures are prudent to prevent encounters, and there are some things to do if the unspeakable happens. Statistics show there is a much greater risk of succumbing from a motor vehicle accident or a heart attack than from a man-eating animal. (Sharks are covered in the Bites section of chapter 3.)

If you encounter a hostile animal, keep your head, and keep your eye on the animal. If you have come across a female with her young, and her response is defensive, play dead. However, if you are charged in an offensive attack, then either maneuver yourself into a position where you can get away, or use aggressive gestures yourself. These can be a direct stare, taking the high ground, standing up straight, looking big, grabbing a rock or limb, raising your fist, and shouting forcefully. I have seen this work!

If the unspeakable happens, and results in the unthinkable, it is probably best not to struggle. People who have survived lion attacks state that the beast should be allowed to chew on an extremity in the hope it will lose interest! When the attack is over, treat as described in the Major Trauma section, above.

NEAR-DROWNING

Toddlers and teenage males are the most vulnerable. Suspect neck injuries in diving situations, and immobilize the neck during rescue if possible. Those accidents occurring in cold water, especially to younger children, offer increased potential for survival. Do not withhold resuscitation attempts; remarkable saves have occurred. Mouth-to-mouth respiration can be started during the water rescue process, if it won't cause delay. We don't know yet whether closed chest compressions should be started in the water.

Once out of the water, place the victim on a level, flat surface and continue CPR. The concepts of trying to drain the lungs and to use the Heimlich maneuver (see below) to empty the stomach have no clear-cut utility. The latter might be attempted if the stomach is swollen and interferes with attempts to do mouth-to-mouth respiration. Trying to evacuate seawater from the mouth and throat is probably useful, but precedence should be given to continuing CPR. Warm the patient, and remember that no one is dead until they are warm and dead. Read the Cold Injury, Hypothermia, and Frostbite section in chapter 5. Transport to a facility is required for everyone, including those fortunate ones who seem to have recovered very quickly.

FIRES

The following information is specifically oriented toward a fire in a hotel, the most likely possibility for travelers. The principles of escape, however, apply to fires in any enclosed space.

The broken record again states that prevention is the key. Especially when checking into a hotel, survey the area where you will be spending time, usually your room, and see where the emergency stairways are located. Try to remember the floor plan, since during a fire you probably would not be able to see the signs. Don't smoke in bed.

If you suspect a fire, call the hotel operator or building switchboard and call the fire department. If there are no telephones, shout for help. When there is smoke, get close to the floor. If you leave your room, keep your room key in case you must retreat. If you have time, dress in loose but closely woven cotton, wool, or natural fabrics (not synthetics). Wear long pants and boots and carry a long-sleeved shirt and jacket. Take gloves and goggles, if available, a wet handkerchief to shield the face, and extra water. Before moving into another room, check to see if the door to it is hot or cool. If hot, do not open it. If cool, you can proceed on your hands and knees. Try to avoid going from a less smoky area to one with more fumes. Try to get to a stairwell, entering only if the door to it feels cool. Descend if it is not smoky, but if you encounter smoke, return to the previous room or area. Do not use elevators. You might be instructed to ascend to the roof, but do this only if you have been told to.

If you are stuck in a room and unable to proceed, shut all doors firmly. If possible, fill any large containers (e.g., bathtub) with cold water. Turn all heating and air conditioning units off. Soak towels, clothes, and sheets with cold water and stuff into cracks in the doorway, ventilation ducts, or any openings inside. Open windows to the outside, but do not break them. If fresh air comes in the window and there is smoke in the room, try opening a vent in the bathroom to see if the smoke can clear. If the area outside the window is smoky, open it a crack and hang out a sheet or something to alert rescuers. If you have the option of being in several rooms and one fills with smoke, retreat to another and close the door.

If overtaken by fire, wear all your clothes and lie face down in an area less likely to burn. Jumping without a safety net below is tantamount to suicide. If you are close to the ground, however, you might try fashioning a sturdy line to the bottom. Take comfort in knowing that in major hotel fires, guests who followed these instructions survived!

CHOKING

Foreign bodies, usually food, lodged in the throat or inhaled into the larynx can cause life-threatening choking. Usually the victim will be in an eating place. As long as he or she seems to be breathing, reassure the person and encourage him or her to continue coughing and breathing while trying to expel the foreign material. The situation is serious if the cough becomes weak and ineffective, and a distressing noise is made with inhalation. Or you might determine that no air is moving, since the victim is unable to speak, breathe, or cough and usually clutches his or her throat. Then you need to act.

For an adult, try to relieve the obstruction by back blows and manual thrusts to the chest or abdomen. A combination of techniques is usually more effective than any one. Specifically, give four rapid, sharp blows over the spine between the shoulder blades. Use the heel of your hand. The victim can be standing, sitting, or lying. If possible, have his head lower than his chest.

Abdominal thrusts, also called the Heimlich maneuver, are performed with the victim standing or sitting as follows. Stand behind the victim as if to give him or her a bear hug. Place your hands together just below (toward the feet) the breastbone, and deliver four quick, upward thrusts. If the victim is lying down, place him or her on his back, straddle the person, place both hands together in the same place below the breastbone, and give a quick upward thrust. The victim can do this to him or herself as well.

Chest thrusts are similar to the abdominal ones, except that the hands are placed over the breastbone as for CPR. This method is useful in advanced pregnancy, when there is little room below the breastbone.

Keep repeating these in whatever order is feasible, until success is achieved. Once breathing is established, remember to remove the object from the mouth to prevent reobstruction.

In children, do not deliver the abdominal thrusts. Also, be careful about blindly sweeping your fingers inside the child's mouth to remove the object. You just might push it farther back. With a small child, begin by placing him or her face down and head low, over your knees. Then deliver four blows between the shoulder blades. If unsuccessful, turn the child over and deliver four chest thrusts. Inspect the mouth by protruding the jaw to see if the foreign body is accessible. If breathing is still not restored, attempt mouth-to-mouth respiration. If that is unsuccessful, repeat the sequence and continue repeating it until breathing returns.

Be aware that the exact sequence and types of methods advised are controversial. However, they do work.

A much more common situation is to have food lodged in the esophagus, wherein the individual has pain or discomfort in the region of the obstruction and can't swallow saliva.In this case, have the victim relax if possible, and usually the bolus will pass into the stomach after an hour or more. If not, and you feel the obstruction is near the throat, try to induce vomiting with your fingers. Failing that, seek help, and *do not* try eating a papaya-type enzyme in the hopes of digesting the food.

DEATH

Almost half of deaths in American travelers are from cardiovascular disease; over half of these occur in Europe and generally among the older population. Injuries account for a quarter of deaths in American travelers, with motor vehicle accidents and drownings the most common cause. Alcohol consumption is often involved in those.

All societies have their own rituals for dealing with the dead and the grieving. If one wishes to participate in these and the end result is burial, cremation, or some other disposal of the remains, it would be prudent to try to certify the death for legal purposes back home. Photograph the body to establish little doubt of the identification. Similarly document the ritual. Get an official of the region, the headman, the governor, or the mayor, to prepare a signed statement as to the events leading to the death and noting the identity of the deceased.

Trying to repatriate the body involves the following obstacles. First the body must be transported to a major city. The embassy or consulate may assist in formalities. In many countries, local airlines will not carry corpses on scheduled flights. You may have to charter an airplane or find other means of conveyance. The various traveler's insurance companies and evacuation services may be able to arrange this. There are no restrictions on importing human remains to the United States if death was not caused by cholera, diphtheria, infectious tuberculosis, plague, yellow fever, or viral hemorrhagic fevers. If one of these was the cause, the remains must be properly embalmed and placed in a hermetically sealed casket. In any case, the remains must be accompanied by a death certificate, identifying the individual and the cause of death. This must be translated into English. Each country has its own export regulations that must be followed. Recognizing how difficult all this would be, you might consider not repatriating the body. This is a difficult individual decision.

7

THE RETURNING TRAVELER

Once you return home, it is important to mention to any doctor you see the illnesses or symptoms you have experienced and where you have traveled, especially if the journey was in the last year or so. If you have been to areas of poor sanitation, have a stool exam for ova and parasites if you continue to have symptoms. If you have had close, prolonged contact with sick people in third-world countries and had a negative tuberculin skin test before the journey, it would be prudent to repeat it. If you have been taking malaria suppression, you might take a therapeutic course of primaquine, especially if you have been in an endemic area for many months.

If you have persistent fevers, weight loss, or continuing diarrhea after your journey, seek medical attention. Fevers in returning travelers are likely to be caused by malaria, typhoid, hepatitis, or another virus. Infection with leptospirosis is a recent concern. Travelers to many third-world countries who spend a long time there in close contact with the local people seem to have some immune system depression afterward that results in illness, especially involving the gastrointestinal tract. Exotic tropical diseases sometimes show up well after you have returned, and you may need to seek a knowledgeable specialist for help.

More likely, having followed the advice in this book, you will be healthy and eager to go again.

Postscript

Thanks to the splendid work of (Dr.) Prone the expedition was remarkably free from illness. All were fit and well, except poor Burley, who had fallen victim to Base Camp lassitude and consequently was not acclimatizing as quickly as the others, and Prone, who was smitten with mysterious and complicated symptoms, namely: pallor, profuse sweating, pulse rapid and soft, temperature sub-normal, deep breathing and sighing, restlessness and thirst, cold extremities, faintness, dizziness and buzzing in the ears. Poor fellow, he was much distressed, both by his condition and by the fact that he was unable to diagnose his ailment. The problem was finally solved by Constant, who produced a first-aid manual and pointed out that the symptoms were exactly those of haemorrhage, except that the first two were missing, namely: insensibility and death. He said there was still hope. Prone then discovered that he had cut himself in the ear while shaving and was slowly bleeding to death. After stopping the bleeding by holding ice against his ear and afterwards treating himself for surgical shock and a frostbitten ear, he went down with Italian measles.

from The Ascent of Rum Doodle by W. E. Bowman

Recommended Reading

Altitude Illness: Prevention and Treatment. Stephen Bezruchka. Seattle: The Mountaineers, 1994. Compact, like this book.

Dive/First Responder. Richard A. Clinchy III. St. Louis, Missouri: Mosby-YearBook, 1996.

Health Information for International Travel (HIFIT). Atlanta, Georgia: Centers for Disease Control, annual. A new edition is published each year in the summer. Single copies are available from the Centers for Disease Control (Attention: Health Information), Center for Prevention Services, Division of Quarantine, Atlanta, GA 30333. It is available online at http://www.cdc.gov/travel/.

Healthy Travel: Bugs, Bites & Bowels. Jane Wilson Howarth. London: Cadogan Books, 1995. Distributed in the United States by Globe Pequot Press. Fun to read and informative.

How to Beat Jet Lag: A Practical Guide for Air Travelers. Dan Oren, Walter Reich, Norman Rosenthal, and Thomas Wehr. New York: Holt, 1993. The details on light treatment.

Hypothermia, Frostbite and Other Cold Injuries. James A. Wilkerson. Seattle: The Mountaineers, 1986. Concise, practical advice.

International Travel and Health: Vaccination Requirements and Health Advice. World Health Organization. Geneva, Switzerland: WHO, 1997. Available at http://www.who.int/ith/.

International Travel Health Guide. Stuart Rose (with Jay Keystone, Phyllis Kozarsky). Northampton, Mass.: Travel Medicine Inc., 1998. Order from (800) 872-8633. Much useful destination specific information, updated yearly.

Medicine for Mountaineering. James A. Wilkerson. Seattle: The Mountaineers, 1992. The standard reference.

The Merck Manual of Medical Information: Home Edition. Robert Berkow. New Jersey: Merck, 1997. A 1,500-page, compact compendium with useful information published by the world's largest pharmaceutical company.

Staying Healthy in Asia, Africa, and Latin America. Dirk Schroeder. Chico, Calif.: Moon, 1995.

Textbook of Travel Medicine. Herbert Dupont and Robert Steffan. Toronto, Ont.: Decker, 1997. A new resource for clinicians containing material not found elsewhere.

The Travel and Tropical Medicine Manual. Elaine Jong and Russell McMullen. Philadelphia: W. B. Saunders, 1995. Written for the medical profession but compact and with a wealth of information to serve as a useful adjunct to this book.

Travelers' Health. Richard Dawood. New York: Random House, 1994. Another source to extend this book.

Travel for the Disabled: A Handbook of Travel Resources and 500 Worldwide Access Guides. Helen Hecker. Portland, Ore.: Twin Peaks Press, 1985.

Traveling Healthy: Health Advice for the Global Traveler. Karl Neumann. A useful monthly newsletter available by subscription from Shoreland, P.O. Box 13795, Milwaukee, WI 53213-0795, (800) 433-5256, (414) 774-4600, E-mail service@shoreland.com, fax (414) 774-4060.

Where There Is No Dentist. Murray Dickson. Palo Alto, Calif.: The Hesperian Foundation, 1983.

Where There Is No Doctor. David Werner. Palo Alto, Calif.: The Hesperian Foundation, 1992. A microfiche copy together with a reader is available from the publisher. Consider carrying the fiche version on your travels as a reference.

Where Women Have No Doctor: A Health Guide for Women. A. August Burns, Ronnie Lovich, Jane Maxwell, and Katharine Shapiro. Berkeley, Calif.: The Hesperian Foundation, 1997. Superbly designed and readable.

Wilderness Medicine: Management of Wilderness and Environmental Emergencies. Paul S. Auerbach. St. Louis, Missouri: Mosby, 1995. Written for the medical professions, but accessible to interested travelers.

Your Child's Health Abroad: A Manual for Travelling Parents. Jane Wilson-Howarth and Matthew Ellis. Old Saybrook, Conn.: Globe Pequot Press, 1998. Written by parents and doctors; contains a wealth of useful advice.

INDEX

About the Author

Stephen Bezruchka has lived and traveled widely in the third world. His wanderlust began before he became a physician. Educated at Harvard, Stanford, and Johns Hopkins Universities, he is a board-certified emergency medicine specialist and teaches in the School of Public Health and Community Medicine of the University of Washington. He tries to disseminate information on the relationship between income distribution and the health of populations. He has provided health care in a remote region of Nepal, has collaborated with that government to turn a rural district hospital into a teaching hospital for Nepali doctors, and now works to improve surgical services in remote district hospitals there. He has climbed in the far ranges of the earth, kayaked and dived in the ocean, bicycled, and hiked. He is a member of the Union International des Associations d'Alpinism Medical Commission, the Wilderness Medical Society, and the International Society of Travel Medicine. He has had giardiasis, ascariasis, and amebiasis, but not recently. Now he practices what he preaches. He is also a member of the Supine Alpine Club, and has suffered from Terminal Torpor, Glacier Lassitude, and HAFE (high altitude flatus expulsion). He is the author of *Trekking in Nepal: A Traveler's Guide, Nepali for Trekkers,* and *Altitude Illness: Prevention and Treatment.*